PSYCHOLOGY AND FAITH:

The Christian Experience of Eighteen Psychologists

Edited by
H. Newton Malony

Graduate School of Psychology
Fuller Theological Seminary

University Press
of America™

Copyright © 1978 by

University Press of America, Inc.™

4710 Auth Place, S.E., Washington, D.C. 20023

ISBN: 0-8191-0621-6

Library of Congress Catalog Card Number: 78-63271

To

Delano M. Goehner
(1936-1971)

And

Gene W. Pfrimmer
(1949-1978)

-Young psychologists of great promise-

Their clinical skills, integrative talents,

Christian faiths

and untimely deaths

will not soon be forgotten.

FOREWORD

"You're a Christian, eh?" the man asked the psychologist. So, what difference does that make?"

Answering that question led me to this book. "What is the difference that being Christian makes in the life of a psychologist?", I asked myself.

"Those psychologists who are Christian can answer this better than anyone else", I mused.

So I went to eighteen of them and asked the question. "Tell me about yourself", I inquired. "How did you decide to become a psychologist? Share your Christian experience. Describe what you do in your daily life. How do you relate your faith with your work? What difference does being Christian make to you?"

This book is their story--the autobiographies of eighteen psychologists who find the meaning of their lives in the revelation of God in Jesus Christ.

The uniqueness of this book lies in its writers -- the psychologists. Many people in our day have heard about psychology. Few people know much about psychologists. And this is especially true of psychologists who are Christian.

We can find books relating faith to work written about doctors, educators, scientists, farmers, architects--even counselors and psychiatrists. Little or nothing has been written about psychologists and their faith.

This is not only a unique but a timely book. Psychology is in vogue. Child rearing, group interaction, social issues, industrial output, courtship and marriage--all are frought with psychological questions. This is the day of psychology. More students major in psychology than any other one subject.

And many of these students are Christians. They are seeking ways to relate their faith to their vocations. "What exactly do psychologists do? Can I be Christian and be a psychologist? Will I be able to express my faith through this career?", they are asking.

i

The answers to these questions are by no means clear or simple. From early times, many psychologists have been openly critical of religion and faith. Finding good illustrations of those who relate their faith to their vocations is not an easy task. Yet,they can be discovered. The psychologists who write here are good examples. And, I have every confidence that they illustrate viable ways any Christians who become psychologists can express their faith through their daily life. I am grateful to the eighteen persons who agreed to share themselves in these pages. They are my colleagues and my friends. It is a privilege to join with them in detailing what it means to be "psychologists" and "Christians" in the twentieth century. I am appreciative and dependent on my secretaries, Carol Burke, Marge Long and Carey Ingle for long hours of tedious typing, dutiful persistence, and extensive patience with an eccentric editor such as myself. Also, appreciation is given to Richard H. Bube, editor of the Journal of American Scientific Affiliation, for permission to reprint part of an article entitled "The Psychologist Christian" which appeared in that Journal in 1972, Vol. 24 (4), pp.135-144.

H. Newton Malony
Pasadena, California
1978

TABLE OF CONTENTS

CONTRIBUTORS

Walter Houston Clark, A.M., Ph.D., Professor of the
    Psychology of Religion, Retired, Andover Newton
    Theological Seminary.

Gary R. Collins, Ph.D. Professor of Pastoral
    Counseling and Psychology, Trinity-Evangelical
    Divinity School, Deerfield, Illinois.

Paul W. Clement, M.A., Ph.D., Professor and Director
    of the Psychology Center, Graduate School of
    Psychology, Fuller Theological Seminary.

James E. Dittes, M.Div., Ph.D. Professor of The
    Psychology of Religion and Director of Graduate
    Studies in Religion, Yale University.

John G. Finch, B.D., Ph.D., Private Practice in
    Clinical Psychology, Tacoma, Washington and
    Visiting Professor, Graduate School of Psycho-
    logy, Fuller Theological Seminary.

William H. Fitts, Ph.D., Director of Research, Dede
    Wallace Center, Private Practice of Clinical
    Psychology, Nashville, Tennessee.

Richard L. Gorsuch, M.Div., Ph.D. Professor Social
    Work of Psychology, University of Texas at
    Arlington.

Robert W. Hites, M.A., Ph.D., Director of Admissions,
    University of North Carolina at Greensboro.

Richard A. Hunt, B.D., Ph.D., Professor of Psychology
    and Director of Psychological Services, Southern
    Methodist University.

H. Newton Malony, M.Div., Ph.D., Professor and
    Director of Programs in the Integration of
    Psychology and Theology, Graduate School of
    Psychology, Fuller Theological Seminary.

Mary Jo Meadow, Ph.D., Associate Professor, College
    of Social and Behavioral Sciences, Mankato State
    University, Mankato, Minnesota.

Billy B. Sharpe, B.D., Ed.D., Director, W. Clement
    Stone Foundation and Achievement Motivation
    Systems, Chicago, Illinois.

Orlo Strunk, Jr., STM., Ph.D., Professor of The
    Psychology of Religion, Boston University
    School of Theology.

F. Fagan Thompson, B.D., Ph.D., Chief of The
    Psychology Department, Rusk State Hospital,
    Rusk, Texas.

Lee Edward Travis, M.A., Ph.D., Dean Emeritus and
    Distinguished Professor of Psychology, Graduate
    School of Psychology, Fuller Theological Seminary.

Donald F. Tweedie, Ph.D., Private Practice of Clinical
    Psychology, Hacienda Heights, California.

John Monroe Vayhinger, B.D., Ph.D., Professor of
    Psychology and Pastoral Care, The School of
    Theology, Anderson College.

Neil Clark Warren, M.Div., Ph.D., Dean and Associate
    Professor, Graduate School of Psychology,
    Fuller Theological Seminary.

Jack E. Wiersma, Ed.D., Professor of Psychology,
    Calvin College, Grand Rapids, Michigan.

FAITH AND VOCATION

Vocational choice is always a combination of the situation and the person. Many vocational theorists have put an emphasis on the "market place". They have suggested that most persons choose their work on the basis of what is available at the time they go looking for a job. However, to overstress the importance of the environment is to ignore several more personal aspects of vocational choice. To begin with, many jobs require prior preparation. Persons have to decide to enter a vocation and take training before they go looking for jobs. Again, self-conscious identity often determines which jobs are attractive and which are not. Erik Erikson illustrates this in his account of the life of Martin Luther. His understanding of himself as a child of the church led him into a priestly vocation. Finally, the emerging norm of entering several vocations during a lifetime cannot be ignored. As persons experience their careers their interests change. Often, this leads to vocations in new or related fields.

Certainly, the interplay of faith in all these issues is crucial but subtle. For persons such as psychologists one might expect their faith to influence the choice to enter psychology and the work they do from day to day.

This first chapter is an introduction to these faith-vocation dynamics in the lives of psychologists who are Christian.

H. Newton Malony is Professor and Director of
Programs in the Integration of Psychology and
Theology in the Graduate School of Psychology of
Fuller Theological Seminary. In addition to being
a clinical psychologist, he is also an ordained
United Methodist minister. He is interested in
helping churches become more affective organizations
and his research is focused in the psychology of
religion. He has published such books as Religious
experience: Its nature and function in the human
psyche (with Walter H. Clark). The nature of man:
A social psychological perspective (with Richard L.
Gorsuch, and Current perspectives in the psychology
of religion. He is a diplomate in clinical psychology,
the American Board of Professional Psychology.

The Psychologist-Christian
by
H. Newton Malony

"Calling" or "vocation" means primarily the
call to acknowledge a relationship to God, and
to live in responsible obedience to Him where-
ever one is. Hence it also means a call to a
particular task, and response to God in one's
daily work.   1

The beliefs of the psychologists cannot affect
his findings unless he actually cheats, so that
there is no special kind of psychologist known
as a "Christian Psychologist"--that would
simply be a psychologist who happens to hold
certain beliefs.   2

The two authors quoted above take contradictory
points of view. The first, Ian Barbour, implies that
religious faith and particular vocation are integrally
related--for the Christian person. The second, Michael
Argyle, proposes that a definite distinction exists
between what one does for a living and the religious beliefs one holds. I believe Barbour is correct and
Argyle is wrong--but this has yet to be demonstrated
for psychologists.

There is a need therefore to detail first, who
psychologists are; second, who Christians are; and
finally, how psychologists who are Christians coordi-
nate their profession with their faith.

Who are the Psychologists

Psychology is comparatively new. Although
Melanchthon coined the term "psychology" in the early
1500's [3], it was not recognized as a separate discipline
from philosophy until the late 1800's. Wilhelm Wundt
established the first psychological laboratory in 1879
at the University of Leipzig. By the end of the next
decade James McKeen Cattell had been appointed the first
Professor of Psychology in America and Joseph Jastrow
had been awarded this country's first Ph.D. degree in
psychology. Before the turn of the century, William
James had written his popular Principles of Psychology,
the American Psychological Association had been organized, and the first psychological clinic had been opened.

3

Psychology has grown rapidly. The American Psychological Association began with thirty-one members. It now includes over 39,000 members. The National Science Foundation reported in1968 that approximately one in twelve scientists was a psychologist.[4] Many students aspire to careers in psychology, as is evident by the more than 2000 doctoral and 5000 masters degrees in psychology awared each year.

There has been numerous attempts to define psychology, one widely agreed upon definition is that psychology is that "... scholarly discipline, . . . scientific field, and , , , professional activity which studies animal and human behavior".[5] Behavior could be defined as the psychological reactions, the feelings, the thoughts, the words and the outward actions of people and animals. Normal, abnormal, individual and interpersonal behaviors are of interest to psychologists.

Psychology has become a scholarly discipline in that the principles of "behavior" are a major field of study in colleges and universities. Psychology has become a science in that it utilizes research methods to investigate behavior and draws conclusions on the basis of empirical results. Psychology has become a profession in that it applies its knowledge of behavior in efforts to resolve individual and social problems.

However, modern psychology is unified in that it possesses a vast literature on individual and social behaviors; a broad understanding of human development from infancy to old age; many techniques for working with individuals and groups; must new knowledge about physiological functioning; refined mathematical and statistical techniques and numerous methods for applying its knowledge to industry, society and education.

While all psychologists hold the MA or the Ph.D. degree, they have varied interests and skills and they work in many different types of locations. They can be found in schools, colleges and universities, clinics and hospitals, governmental and welfare agencies, industry, business and in the public health service. Some are even self-employed.

Types of Psychologists

The many types of psychologists can be seen in the thirty-one divisions of the American Psychological

4

Association. Among them are the divisions of clinical, counseling, experimental, educational, school, engineering, and physiological psychology.

The largest single group of psychologists are known as clinical psychologists. They comprise twenty-one per cent of the total membership of the American Psychological Association. The term "clinical" was coined in the early 1930's by Ligntner Witmer to designate a type of psychologist who works with persons in the assessment and resolution of their emotional and adjustment problems. Thus most clinical psychologists are professionals in the sense that they apply principles of behavior.

They are not psychiatrists as some presume, however. They use non-medical means, such as counseling and behavior modification, to change behavior and to solve persons' problems. Clinical psychologists often function as academicians and scientists also. They teach and conduct research. They are most often found in schools, hospitals, mental health centers, colleges and in private practice.

Another significant group of psychologists are known as experimental psychologists. The term is frequently reserved for those who conduct basic research in behavioral processes. Most often this is done in laboratories connected with academic institutions. Nevertheless, many experimentalists are becoming somewhat professional in that they are consulting with businesses and industries. For example, the design of industrial machines to best fit the capabilities of the men who run them is known as the field of engineering psychology. Most engineering psychologists are experimental psychologists functioning in a professional role.

Numerous other types of psychologists could be discussed. However, there is a growing opinion among psychologists that there is in reality only one type of psychologist, not many. While their interest in various areas of behavior may differ, they all are in agreement that the empirical study of basic behavioral processes provides the foundation for applied efforts to change behavior. Further, while a given psychologist may spend more or less time in consultation or basic research, they all retain primary interest in persons and their problems.

5

In summary, psychologists are academicians, scientists, and professionals who attempt to understand and influence behavior in all of its manifestations. While persons have always studied each other's actions, psychology has only recently been recognized as a separate discipline and thus persons known as psychologists have been in existence only a little more than seventy-five years.

Who are the Christians?

Just as there have been numerous attempts to define psychology, so have there been many definitions of Christianity. Perhaps the simple assertion that a Christian is one who has faith in Jesus Christ would receive common approval even if there was disagreement over its implication. The greek word for "fish"-- "Icthus"-- used by early Christians, sums up this definition. The letters stand for the simple statement of faith that He is "Jesus Christ, Son of God, Savior".

There would probably also be wide agreement with the statement that a person's Christian faith should have an effect on what he or she does. Being a Christian involves, therefore, action as well as belief. The belief or faith in Jesus Christ supposedly influences the actions and daily work of the Christian. This is as it should be, in spite of the fact that one study reported that over half the persons interviewed indicated no felt relationship between their faith and their vocation.[6]

The Christian life involves an important emphasis on behavior as well as faith. The Christian is one who has faith and does work. The rhythm of the Christian life moves back and forth between worship, which renews faith, and work, which expresses faith. As has been said, ". . . the Christian finds himself moving between his sources in Christ and his services in the world".[7]

The emphasis is subsumed under the Christian doctrine of "vocation" or "calling". In times past, "talling" has been a term applied only to those who became ministers or pastors. This is a misunderstanding of the issue. It is the Christian conviction that all men are called to live by their faith in God through Christ which gives them the understanding that they are the children of God. This is the Christian calling.

6

All persons are called upon to the Christian life. As
Paul LeFevre suggested:

> Christians are "called". They are called to
> the Christian life, to a Christian vocation
> in a larger sense, at the same time that
> they may feel themselves to be called to some
> specialized vocation such as law, medicine,
> preaching or teaching. A particular pro-
> fession can be a calling from God only be-
> cause it is possible to exercise the more
> general calling, that of living the Chris-
> tian life, within it.   8

Thus the Christian vocation is the same for every person.
It is a vocation of living life as a child of God in
whatever occupation one assumes.

Four biblical metaphors which have been used to
describe the vocation of the Christian are: Servant,
Light, Salt and Soldier.[9] They are offered here as a
possible model for our later discussion of the psychologist-Christian.

Servant

Jesus pictured Himself as a Servant and often encouraged His followers to follow Him in serving their
fellow men (Mark 10:43-44). Thus, the first way of
working out one's calling is to be a servant. Matthew
25:40 explicitly suggests that to meet the needs of a
neighbor is to serve God. To be a servant includes
several facets. Phillippians implies that it should
include a love for people, require sacrifice of oneself,
be based on identifying with the needs of others and
results in direct help.

Light

The second metaphor for Christian action is Light.
"You are the light of the world", Jesus told His followers (Matthew 5:14). The implication is that the Christian, by his/her goodness, is to lead others to faith
in Christ. It implies that Christians will behave in
such a manner that others will admire them and/or inquire as to their motives. In all experiences they
will relate themselves to their faith. They will attempt
to live out or incarnate the implications of their
faith.

7

Salt

Salt is the third term for Christian behavior.
Jesus told His followers that they were the "salt of
the earth" (Matthew 5:13). Salt suggests seasoning.
Seasoning makes food taste better by permeation. The
emphasis here is on active participation in the world.
Thus, Christians are not ascetic but secular in the
fullest sense of the word. They are involved and enthusiastic in non-religious affairs outside the church.
Like salt scattered over meat, so Christians are dispersed over the activities of the modern world. In
these events the Christian will be working toward making things become as they should be.

Soldier

The last metaphor for the Christian life is that
of Soldier (II Timothy 2:3-4). Soldiering involves
active efforts to make Christ the Lord of activities and
situations. It also involves a willingness to suffer
when success does not come easily. This aspect of the
work of the Christian implies that they are in tension
with their environment and are engaged in a struggle to
change things. The old hymn "Onward Christian Soldiers"
speaks of many of these issues. Soldiers of Christ encounter the world and join their fellows within the
church in changing the world in the name of Christ.

These four, therefore, are qualities of the Christian's behavior. They are metaphors rather than concrete prescriptions because the precise acts of Christians are impossible to predict. This difficulty is
similar to the question of whether Christians can be
found in this or that occupation. It is now agreed
that all Christians are called to live the Christian
life and that any occupation which allows persons to
exercise their calling as children of God is acceptable.
This was certainly Martin Luther's intent in his doctrines of "vocation" and the "priesthood of all believe
rs". Work is what Christians do to fulfill their calling.

Who are the Psychologist-Christians?

Whether or not one is Christian might be expected
to influence one's choice of work within a chosen
occupation. Five ways in which the Christian faith could
be expressed in the life of a psychologist have been
proposed.[10] Psychologists can integrate their faith

8

1) intrapersonally, 2) professionally or scientifically; 3) experimentally; 4) theoretically; and 5)
interprofessionally. These five provide a convenient
model for considering the ways in which being Christian might influence the vocation of being a psychologist.

Intrapersonal Integration

Intrapersonal integration refers to the influence
of faith on vocational choice and on beliefs. As
Christians, it would be important for persons to feel
that by becoming psychologists they could obey God's
call to be His children. As LeFevre notes:

> Should we feel that we could no longer be
> Christians within our particular profession
> or that we could better exercise our re-
> sponsibility as Christians within another
> calling, other things being equal, we would
> feel a strong inward pressure to relinquish
> our present work and to seek some other. [11]

Thus, we might expect to find persons who in part chose
to become psychologists because it is a means by which
they would fulfill their Christian calling.

Another aspect of intrapersonal integration would
be in the area of personal belief. One would expect to
find among psychologist-Christian persons for whom faith
continued to be a live option and persons whose faith
was well integrated with their own learnings in psychology. While their faith would not be free from doubt,
they would nevertheless have come to some basic resolution of the science-religion issue.

The metaphor that comes closest to expressing this
type of integration is that of Light. The psychologist's
personal faith remains vital for him/her as he/she
chooses psychology as an avenue for expressing the calling to be a child of God. One thus has motivations
which bring new insight or Light into his/her life.
Possibly others see this and inquire of him/her regarding it.

However, a point of tension comes at the time when
the psychologist experiences doubt and confusion.
These experiences come to all people. It is difficult
to hold on to faith in ultimate meaning and justice
and goodness in the face of the modern world. This is
the Christian-psychologist's problem just as it is

9

everybody's dilemma. More pointedly, to the psychologist Christian the problems of religion and science are very personal. Also in dealing with troubled people he/she must face the tragedy of mental illness. Personal faith does not come easy or stay without effort for the Christian psychology. The tension is great.

Professional Integration

The second type of integration of faith and vocation is in the practice of one's vocation.[12] Since psychology has been designated a profession, a science and an academic discipline, this would mean integration of the Christian faith with professional tasks, scientific endeavors, and soberly activities. This pertains to the influence of faith on activities within a vocation.

No doubt the classic metaphor for day-to-day activity within the Christian life is that of Servant. Other people and their needs are important. The Christian is to respond to others by being good to his/her neighbor, i.e. by loving mercy and doing justly (Micah 6:8). This is Christian service. The actual meaning of this on the job becomes the problem for as has been said, "Being a Christian geologist does not mean finding oil on church property. It means serving God and man in the daily work of Geology."[13]

At one level, working in a religious setting such as a church college or hospital or seminary could be considered an example of this type of integration.

Of course, the content of a person's work is probably more important than the context. What the psychologist-Christian does is more crucial than where he/she does it. Further, the integration of faith and profession should refer to the teaching, consulting, and researching activities of psychologists as well as the more obviously service-related tasks of counseling.

The metaphor of Soldier probably best fits this activity of the psychologist-Christian in that she/he is actively pursuing, through research and study, the God-given task of transcending the world through knowledge which makes persons less subject to finitude and makes them more able to relate to the Divine.

Overall, the integration of faith in professional, scientific and academic practice could be understood through the metaphor of Salt. In a wide variety of tasks, psychologist-Christians attempting this type of integration are, indeed, seasoning their situations with their faith.

Once again, the task is not an easy one. Although many saints have seen their daily tasks as God-given, the average person finds it difficult, if not im-possible, to discover such meaning in their work. Daily tasks are often experienced as neutral at best or meaningless at worst. The Christian-psychologist has to work at keeping faith at the center of work - just as everyone else has to. Although clinical or counseling psychologists work with people (and thus could find Christian meaning in that task) many other psychologists engage in less dramatic tasks. Being sure of one's faith in the midst of one's vocational role is an ongoing dilemma for these persons.

Experimental Integration

Integration through research in the psychology of religious behavior is a third means by which the in-fluence of faith might be expressed in the work of the psychologist. There is a long tradition of such in-terest beginning with G. Stanley Hall's extensive surveys of religious conversions in adolescents. [14] William James Stanley provided such interest in the field with his 1902 Gifford Lectures [15] that a journal in the area, the <u>Journal of Religious Psychology and Education</u>,[16] was published.Dittes reports that almost one-fourth of the presidents of the American Psycho-logical Association have evidenced concern with the study of religion at some point in their careers. [17]

These efforts could be conceived as "faith seek-ing understanding", in the words of Augustine. The behavior of these psychologist-Christians could be understood under the metaphor of Light in that they illuminate religious experience through their efforts.

Yet, when research on religion is undertaken there is the constant temptation to treat faith as just another object of study. Some research has found, in fact, that scholars who study religion are less likely to be personally religious than others who do not. Faith becomes objective and sterile for those who study it - or at least it can become so. There is another pitfall for religious researchers. This is that they will come to the place where they no longer know how to ask the right questions of their data. The study of faith is probably best done from inside the faith by those who remain religious in the midst of their academic tasks. Keeping faithful while one is a student of religion is a constant point of tension for the psychologist-Christian.

Conceptual-Theoretical Integration

A closely related type of integration to research in the psychology of religion is conceptual-theoretical integration. Theologians such as Paul Tillich [18] and Albert Outler [19] addressed themselves to this but few psychologists have done so. Among those who did so were early writers such as William James (The Varieties of Religious Experience, 1902) and G. Stanley Hall (Jesus, the Christ in the Light of Psychology, 1917). Through the years others have written on these issues (e.g. James H. Leuba, Robert Thouless, William McDougall, and Walter Houston Clark).[20] More recently John Finch has attempted an explication of[21] psychological theory for the Christian view of man and Hobart Mowrer has analyzed the distortion of theology by psychological theory.[22] Further, other writers have considered religious myths and guilt, religion and existentialism, mental health and salvation, and the relationships between psychological and theological methods.[23] These are indices of how psychologists might express their faith through conceptual or theoretical efforts to integrate their faith and their science. Theorizing, like research requires in interest as a motivating factor. As has also been said in regard to research, the metaphor of Light is appropriate here, too, as indicative of the type of Christian action involved. This is also faith seeking understanding.

Nevertheless, here, too, is a crucial area of concern for the psychologist who would be Christian. There is the ever present danger of reducing religion to science or vice versa. The balance is precarious and difficult. Often the theoretician goes one way or the other, i.e. sees the issues only through the eyes of psychology or through the eyes of religion. It is awesome thing for human beings to put their science or their faith into concepts. Psychologist-Christians know the problems and undertake the task with some trepidation. They wrestle with these issues again and again.

Interprofessional Integration

The last mode of integration is that of inter-professional relationships. This refers to relation-ships psychologists have with religious institutions and religious professionals. This is exemplified by a willingness to consult with churches and to confer with pastors. Many ministers refer persons to psychologists for counseling.

Some psychologists have tried to analyze church behavior through psychological categories. James Dittes has written a psychodynamic interpretation of the ebh and flow of administering the program of the church,[24] while Robert Hites has summarized the principles of behaviorism as they apply to the tasks of church workers.[25] Paul Barkman analyzed motivations for mis-sionary service among college students.[26] These are forms of indirect interprofessional integration of psychology and religion.

The metaphor that best fits this type of inte-gration is that of Servant because herein the psych-ologist uses her/his skills in service to her/his faith.

However, the role of the interprofessional inte-grator is not an easy one. The psychologist is often lured into feeling superior. Thus, he/she speaks down to church persons as if psychology knew all the answers. Psychologists who integrate with other pro-fessionals know how tempting it is to speak loud and to listen little. Yet the Christian also knows that pastors represent another body of knowledge, i.e. the gospel, which must be listened to. It, in addi-tion to psychology, has much to say about human rela-tionships. How to be a sharer and a listener at the same time is a problem for the inter-professional integrator.

13

Conclusion

Ideally, the vocation of psychology should be an
expression of faith for the Christian person who
chooses this vocation. The four metaphors of Salt,
Soldier, Servant and Light were proposed as types of
faith expression. A number of possible behavioral
indeces of these metaphors were suggested. The critical
question is, "Have we fully enumerated these behaviors
or even determined the necessity of one of the listed
behaviors for the life of the psychologist-Christian?"
I think the answer to the above question must be "no"
for three reasons.

Religionless Christianity

First, the ideas of Dietrich Bonhoeffer, among
others, regarding "religionless Christianity",[27] have
influenced many other persons. Many intellectuals,
psychologists among them, have become impatient with
organized religion. Thus, they may have intentionally
chosen to be overtly non-religious out of Christian
conviction. This is paradoxical. These persons who
express their faith in non-religious ways would not
evidence integration of the types referred to in this
essay but might at the same time be psychologist-
Christians. They might not be church-persons, work in
religious settings or show interest in the psychology
of religion but might be faithing persons nevertheless.

Behavior and Motivation

Second, there always remains the problem between
behavior and motivation. Jesus Himself spoke of foolish
generations which looked for signs. Richard Smith
represents some modern theologians who suggest that,
" . . . the manifestation of faith is not simple, but
dialectical".[28] By dialectical is meant that the in-
ference from behavior to motive is not simple and may,
in fact, be absolutely false. For example, human
intentions always fall prey to the capriciousness of
human life. Therefore, it may be impossible for a person to express his/her faith in many ways mentioned
here. More important, the Christian faith is itself an
affirmation of hope in the face of meaninglessness.
Therefore faith may be present more in weakness than
in strength and more in the absence of a minifesta-
tion than in its presence.

Christian theology has noted that the forgiveness of sin is a greater reality than the power to

14

express one's faith. This does not mean that faithing persons should resign themselves to futility or libertarianism. Nevertheless it is a recognition that the absence of an overt sign of relationship between the Christian faith and the life of the psychologist may not indicate a lack of faith at all. Thus, our overt indices would be insensitive to these dialectical distinctions. We might find psychologist-Christians witnessing to their faith in the way they handle failure or suffering; in their persistence at hum-drum tasks and meaningless duties; and in their human solutions for administrative and research problems.

Autobiography is Important

Instead of judging overt indices of faith, one would need to inquire of a given psychologist as to his/her own unique expression of faith. The implication is that ultimately a person's behavior makes sense to that person regardless of its consistency in the eyes of others. Comparing a person to others or to standards is far less important than assessing the degree to which that person sees himself/herself as integrated around his/her own values. The psychologist-Christian, therefore, must best be understood from within or by listening to them reflect on the relationship of faith and vocation in their own terms. No doubt autobiographies are the best method for accomplishing this goal and such gross measures as have been discussed herein must pale in importance in comparison to such data.

In conclusion, there is a need to reaffirm confidence in the effect of faith on daily work. As has been suggested earlier, in the Christian faith:

> "Calling" or "vocation" means primarily the call to acknowledge a relationship to God, and to live in responsible obedience to Him wherever one is. Hence, it also means a call to a particular task, and response to God in one's daily work. [29]

The Christian lives life as a response. If, by chance the Christian is a psychologist, that part of his/her life will be no different. It, too, will be a response and, thus, the activities engaged in will be influenced by his/her faith.

15

Points of Tension

In the self reports that follow most, if not all,
of the key points of tension in living Christianity as
a psychology will be addressed. Look for these authors
to wrestle with questions like these.

- How does one's Christian faith help in counseling
  troubled people?

- Is it possible to remain religious while one does
  research on religious experience?

- Are drugs a legitimate tool for use in studying
  religious faith?

- Can one teach scientific psychology in a public
  university and still remain a Christian?

- Is there a spiritual dimension in modern
  psychology?

- Must one convert a person to Christianity in
  psychotherapy?

- Does God work in ways we do not recognize or
  call by name?

- Is modern psychology the enemy of religion?

- How does faith relate to such varied activities as
  being a psychologist in a state hospital to being
  an administrator in a university?

- Do Christian psychologists still have vital religious experiences?

- Can a psychologist be a behaviorist and a Christian at the same time?

- Is there room for the freedom of man in modern
  psychology?

- To very personal answers let us now turn.

FOOTNOTES

[1] Barbour, 1960, p. 13

[2] Argyle, 1958, p. 22

[3] LaPointe, 1970

[4] National Science Foundation, 1968

[5] American Psychological Association, 1970

[6] Wentz, 1963

[7] Wentz, 1963, p. 66

[8] LeFevre, 1958, p. 14

[9] Wentz, 1963

[10] Clement, 1969

[11] LeFevre, 1958, p. 14

[12] Clement, 1969

[13] Barbour, 1960, p. 11

[14] Hall, 1891-1904

[15] James, 1961

[16] Hall, 1905

[17] Dittes, 1969

[18] Tillich, 1952

[19] Outler, 1954

[20] Leuba, 1912; Thouless, 1923, McDougall, 1934, Clark,1958

[21] Finch, 1967

[22] Mowrer, 1961

[23] Pruyser, 1964, 1965; Royce, 1962; Rogers, 1968; Havens, 196

[24] Dittes, 1967

[25] Hites, 1965

[26] Barkman, 1969

[27] Bonhoeffer, 1955

[28] Smith, 1966, p. 55

[29] Barbour, 1960, p. 13

REFERENCES

American Psychological Association. A Career in Psychology. Washington D.C.: American Psychological Association, 1970 A.

Argyle, M. Religious Behaviour. Glencoe, Illinois: The Free Press, 1958.

Barbour, I.C. Christianity and the Scientist. New York: Association Press, 1960.

Barkman, P.E. Christian Collegians and Foreign Missons, An Analysis of Relationships. Monrovia, California: Missions Advanced Research and Communication Center, 1969.

Bonhoeffer, D. Ethics. New York: The Macmillan Co. 1955.

Clark, W.H. The Psychology of Religion. New York: MacMillan, 1958.

Clement, P. Integration of psychology and therapy in theory, research, and practice. Newsletter, Corresponding Committee of Fifty, Division 12, APA. 1969, 6(11), 12-19.

Dittes, J.E. The Church in the Way. New York: Scribners, 1967.

Dittes, J.E. Psychology of Religion. In C. Lindsey and E. Aronson, The Handbook of Social Psychology, 2nd edition. Reading, Massachusetts: Addison Wesley, 1969, 602-659.

Finch, J. Toward a Christian Psychology. Insight: Interdisciplinary studies of man. 1967, 6(1), 42-48.

Hall, G.S. (Ed.) Editorial. Journal of Religious Psychology and Education, 1905, 1, 1-7.

Havens, J. The participant's v.s. the observer's frame of reference in the psychological study of religion. Journal for the Scientific Study of Religion, 1964, 3, 216-226.

Hites, R.W. The Act of Becoming. New York: Abingdon Press, 1965.

James, W. *Principles of Psychology*. New York: Holt, 1890.

James, W. *The Varieties of Religious Experience*. New York: The New American Library, 1961.

La Pointe, F.H. Origin and evaluation of the term "psychology". American Psychologist, 1970, <u>25</u> (7) 640-646.

Leuba, J.H. *A Psychological Study of Religion*. New York: Macmillan, 1912.

McDougall, W. *Religion and the Sciences of Life*. Durham, North Carolina: Duke University Press, 1934.

Mowrer, O.H. *The Crisis in Psychiatry and Religion*. New York: Van Nostrand, 1961.

National Science Foundation. Summary of American Science Manpower, 1968. Washington, D.C.: U.S. Government Printing Office, 1970.

Outler, A. *Psychology and the Christian Message*. New York: Harper & Row, 1954.

Pruyser, P. Anxiety, guilt and shame in atonement. *Theology Today*, 1964, <u>21</u>, 15-33.

Rogers, W.R. Order and class in psychopathology and ontology: a challenge to traditional correlations of order to mental health and ultimate reality, and of chaos to mental health and alienation. In P. Homan's (Ed.) *The Dialogue Between Theology and Psychology*. Chicago: University of Chicago Press, 1968, 249-262.

Royce, J.R. Psychology, existentialism and religion. *Jounral of General Psychology*, 1962, <u>55</u>, 3-16.

Smith, R.G. *Secular Christianity*. New York: Harper and Row, 1966.

Thouless, R.N. *Introduction to the Psychology of Religion*. New York: The Macmillan Co. 1923.

Tillich, P. The Courage to Be, New Haven, Connecticut:
     Yale University Press, 1952.

Wentz, F. K. The Layman's Role Today. New York:
     Abingdon Press, 1963.

II.

THE JOURNEY FROM MINISTRY TO PSYCHOLOGY
(AND VICE VERSA)

As noted earlier, it is not at all common these days to find persons changing vocations in mid-career. In fact, it is estimated that having more than one vocation will become the normal and expected thing for the next generation.

Richard A. Hunt illustrates this trend. He began his career as a minister in the United Methodist Church. In his essay he tells the exciting story of his decision to become a psychologist. By no means does he feel that by becoming a psychologist he rejected the Christian ministery. In fact for him, psychology is an extension of ministry.

Cary R. Collins illustrates the reverse of this phenomenon. He never was an ordained minister but now sees his role of psychologist as a ministry for him. He teaches pastoral counseling to ministerial students in a theological seminary and writes books that help persons relate psychology to their Christian faith.

Together these writers depict the manifold ways in which ministry and psychology go together.

Richard A. Hunt is a counseling psychologist and an ordained United Methodist minister. He is Professor of Psychology at Southern Methodist University in Dallas, Texas, and is Executive Director of Ministry Inventories, Inc. He has four main interests:

First, he has focused on career and marriage counseling for young adults.

Second, he has emphasized marriage enrichment. He recently published the second edition of Creative Marriage (with Edward J. Rydman).

Third, he has been interested in motivation for ministry and has been a prime developer of the Theological School Inventory and author of Ministry and Marriage.

Fourth, he has been a partner with Morton B. King in research in the dimensions of religiosity in America.

Dr. Hunt is a Diplomate in Counseling Psychology, The American Board of Professional Psychology.

A VOCATIONAL JOURNEY

By

Richard A. Hunt

A journey can be marked by "clock-time" (chrones) and "meaning-time" (kairos). Although my vocational development can be seen in the chronology of the hours and days I spend in doing the work of a psychologist, I would like for the dynamic meanings of these events to come to you as they do to me.

A few basic biographical statements provide the context of my vocational journey. For over thirteen years I have been a faculty member of the SMU Psychology Department. During eight and a half of these years, I served as Director of the SMU Counseling Center, and I created and for three years directed the M.A. in Counseling Psychology program. I currently teach courses in the psychology of marriage, introduction to counseling, and marriage and family counseling.

In these settings I have had opportunity to have daily contact with young adults who are not only seeking additional knowledge but are also making important decisions that influence them and the world. In teaching, counseling, and research my focus is upon the development of the persons with whom I work. Often this begins with students discussing problems that are of immediate concern to them. Some have situational concerns, such as being confused by the many alternative lifestyles that are thrust at them on a college campus, deciding about an academic major or career, or finding a suitable date or marriage partner.

At a more basic level, many students are searching for a viable interpretation of life that will give them a sense of purpose and fulfillment in life. College and graduate study is a kairos, a critical time when an individual separates from her/his

parents, looks more carefully at self and the
world, and begins to put his/her life together in
ways that are more meaningful. During this important developmental period, a person is choosing
vocational, marriage, and life commitments. These
decisions are based upon and exemplify a person's
religious commitment.

Choice is Commitment

When a person decides or chooses between goals,
she/he is making a religious commitment. Every person is religious in this sense, although many would
not consider themselves to be making a religious
commitment when they decide about their career or
partner in marriage. For example, consider two
students who major in chemistry. Both may graduate
from college with high grades and find jobs in the
field of chemistry. One student may use this knowledge to develop more destructive weapons of war
while the other person chooses to use similar knowledge to create a cleaner environment.

The difference between these two students is
not just a matter of which jobs are open, how much
each position pays, or where it is located. The
vital difference is in the awareness of and commitment to specific life goals. This manifests one's
religious commitment. Through their career paths,
each person expresses personal convictions about
self and the world.

Being a psychologist is, for me, a way to express my love for God and my neighbor through my
work with college persons. Through my work I seek
to affirm the tremendous positive potential that
persons have. I hope that our students and faculty
can continually commit themselves to using their
abilities and resources in solving some of the contemporary problems that the world has. I try to be
available to students to assist them to think through
their own conflicts and develop plans and skills to
improve their situations. As they discover for themselves some worthwhile answers, they can also share
them with others.

Teaching is Significant

Among several ways of accomplishing this goal, two are especially significant for me. One of these is my work each semester in our course, "the psychology of marriage". The woman-man dyad offers almost unlimited potential for human development, and for Christians it can be interpreted as the basic Christian community. The skills that partners need in marriage are the same as the goals of Christian living, since one's spouse is one's nearest neighbor. A person's marriage is the real-life laboratory in which she/he can practice skills such as trust, affirmation, care, concern, forgiveness, patience, and kindness. These lead to mutual upbuilding, joy, and confidence as partners join together to commit themselves to God's work in the world. Through special presentations in our large classes and through written materials, small group discussions, and individual activities, students in our psychology of marriage classes can develop the skills and attitudes that will enrich their own marriages and their relationships with their families, friends, and associates.

My other significant teaching work is with our graduate students in our counseling psychology program. For our two year master's program, we seek mature persons who can develop competence in psychological counseling and assessment as well as integrate this training into their own lifestyles. To function well at a professional level a person must combine technical competence, professional ethics, and personal qualities such as warmth, concern, and genuineness. In my contacts with graduate students I can benefit them directly and, through them, perhaps benefit many other persons whom I may never know personally.

Research Directions

As a psychologist in a university setting, research is also an important activity. In addition to testing competing theories and solving practical problems, research is a way to listen to the Creator of the universe. As we carefully observe (or listen to) the phenomena in an experiment or the changes in persons, we begin to comprehend the continuing creative and redemptive activity of God. Research can be another exciting dimension of human development.

My own research has focused primarily upon issues in the psychology of religion, such as the development of scales to measure religious beliefs, the relation between personality and religious variables, and the way in which personal skills and commitment are involved in vocational development and in marriage success. Five recent projects have offered opportunity for me to combine research, counseling, and commitment as a Christian.

For several years Morton B. King, a sociologist and Christian layman, and I have collaborated in studying the multiple dimensions of religious commitment, or religiosity. This work has been published in several articles and in a monograph, Measuring Religious Dimensions.

A second major long-term project has been my involvement with measures of interest and motivation for careers in the ministry. For twelve years I have worked with the Theological School Inventory, a counseling instrument for use with seminary students. A specialized computer scoring service for the TSI and a grant for TSI development and training worships have made it possible to keep research on the TSI up to date and to improve its value for theological students and their counselors. The expansion of this project has recently led to the establishment of Ministry Inventories, a non-profit corporation offering computer scoring of assessment instruments, research services, and publications relating to the professional and family development of ministers and of persons preparing for careers in the ordained ministry.

The third project is the continuing development of a program of vocational exploration and development for persons who are considering the ordained ministry as a career. The opportunity to work with the Division of the Ordained Ministry of the United

26

Methodist Church in this project for pre-seminary
persons continues to be challenging and exciting.

Related to these areas is the opportunity to
provide technical consultation to church boards and
agencies. One example of this fourth project is my
involvement with the feedback and evaluation for ministry measuring instruments that have been developed
by the field education staffs of several seminaries.

A fifth project is the development of practical
instruments for assisting couples as they interface
their marriage with careers in the ministry. A work-
book for couples, Ministry and Marriage, has been
designed especially for this purpose.

Some Background Decisions

Basic to my training as a psychologist is my
Ph.D. in psychology. This is the minimum standard
for teaching in a university and for being licensed
as a psychologist. Subsequent supervision and study
have enabled me to become a Diplomate in Counseling
Psychology, granted by the American Board of Professional Psychology. My interest in marriage and family
led me to obtain additional supervision to become a
clinical member of the American Association of
Marriage and Family Counselors. Other workshops and
continuing education opportunities are necessary to
keep my skills and competencies current.

Before becoming a psychologist, however, I
served for thirteen years as a United Methodist pastor
and associate pastor. The seminary training I obtained has been very valuable in giving broader perspectives to my work as a psychologist. I continue to
be an ordained elder and member of the Central Texas
Annual Conference of The United Methodist Church.
As a member of this conference, I am appointed to the
faculty of S.M.U.

My vocational journey, or career path, has been
a gradual unfolding of important events and choices.
While in college, I was always sure I would go on
to complete seminary work, but I had no clear idea of
exactly what I would do after graduation from seminary.

27

During my third year of seminary, I applied for
work in our Methodist Student Movement/Wesley
Foundation program which at that time was the church's
ministry to college campuses. I left my application
on file and at graduation from seminary decided to
become the associate pastor at a large suburban
United Methodist church. During the summer of my third
year in this position, I served one week as a counselor in a conference youth camp. At a vesper service
on Wednesday of that week, a friend of mine, who was
a campus minister, gave the evening meditation.
During that service I thought, "Someday I would like
to work in a college campus situation of some kind."
This was, at the time, a passing thought much like
many other similar "daydreams" we all have probably
had. The next day there was a special delivery letter
which reached me at camp. When I opened the letter,
I read that the chaplain at my college alma mater had
resigned. Another line in the letter invited me to
accept the position if I wanted it!! That "dreamy
someday" suddenly had already arrived.

After discussing the change with my wife, Joan,
we decided to accept the position as chaplain and
instructor of religion. This gave me the opportunity
to see if my earlier interest in college teaching was
merely an immature desire to stay in school or a
genuine call to enter the ministry of Christian higher
education.

After two years teaching experience, my wife and
I found that our interest in college teaching was
confirmed. I soon had the opportunity to begin graduate work in psychology and to teach in college part-
time during this time. Another surprise (which sometimes is an evidence of God's nearness) came from one
of my psychology professors in the form of an invitation to apply for a fellowship that would assure
completion of my doctoral studies in psychology.
Upon my graduation, I came to the Psychology Department of S.M.U.

In some ways this is not the usual path into the
field of psychology, yet none of my time and experience has been wasted. Each experience deepened my
understanding of myself, of various types of indivi-

28

duals, and of the complex yet beautiful ways in
which God works with us.

An individual may be out of college a few years
and then experience the attraction (or God's calling)
to work in a college setting. My experience suggests
that if a person has the motivation, willingness, ability, and encouragement from spouse and others, he/she
can find ways to secure the additional training that
will be needed for college teaching and to find suitable places to teach. The more important question is
whether the individual is growing and maturing in her/
his self-understanding and relationships with others.
There are many ways to achieve this growth. If a vocation as a psychologist in a college setting is the
best match between your abilities and the world's needs,
then you will be able to find the way to do it. Start
by asking people who know the fiel , and keep exploring and using opportunities that are available to you
now.

Some Faith Perspectives

An individual's faith is the central decision
she/he makes about life. This assumption becomes
the foundation upon which she/he builds a personal
world view. My profession as psychologist offers me
full opportunity to manifest or express my faith in
ways which, although probably more covert and un-
obtrusive, may reach out to persons who find traditional institutional church forms meaningless or
repulsive. Thus my vocation as psychologist is a
kind of outer garment or instrument through which I
can share in the deepest and fullest ways possible
my confidence in God's world and God's people.

Although we wish that each person's verbal statements of intentions and beliefs would match his/her
actual behavior, I think that the more important
issue is an individual's behavior or actions themselves. Eventually our verbal statements are rather
hollow, since God's question to us is, "What have you
done for others?" (This is not unlike the focus of
behavior therapy.) There are some professional persons who verbally deny allegience to the Christian
faith, or perhaps to any organized religion, yet

29

these persons are constantly engaged in professional efforts to help others. "By their fruits we will know them."

Any person in any career must continually wrestle with this inner voice of commitment to the highest means and ends we know as humans. It is not an easy task, not is it a task that is resolved once and for all. Ten years from now I expect to be in similar work, but I must remain open to the God-of-the-Future-becoming-Present who may confirm or change my expectations.

I cannot overemphasize the importance of others in one's vocational journey. In my own case, parents, pastors, teachers, friends, and colleagues have been influential for me, often in ways of which they were unaware. For persons who are married, one's spouse is perhaps the major continuing influence on voca-tional directions. My wife of over twenty-seven years, Joan, has continued to encourage and support my voca-tional development in many ways. In today's world of tensions and competition, there is no finer rela-tionship than to have the confidence that there is at least one person who will accept him/her just as one is, without any reservations. This is sublimely expressed in the wedding vows of Christians. Nothing can take the place of a spouse's warm encouragement through graduate education, vocational dilemmas, frustrations, and the excitement and joy of daily professional work.

Being trained both as a minister and a psycholo-gist has been an advantage. It is desirable for every Christian to be trained in both a career field and in the Christian faith. The Christian actually does have "one foot in heaven." As a variety of ancient and modern Christian statements have emphasized, we are citizens of both this world and of the Kingdom of God. A Christian, like any other person, must meet the high standards of educational preparation and train-ing in order to gain entry into a trade or profes-sional area and thus have opportunity through it to express her/his faith. In addition, the Christian must also have a quality education in faith, church, Christian heritage, and other religious areas. Both types of preparation are needed.

My concept of God helps me to clarify the meanings of my life events. Consider an example (or
parable). We do not really know exactly what an individual is, yet we call our friends by their names
and are usually quite clear about whom we are speaking. We could avoid calling them by name by referring to them as 'that influence' or 'important person
number three'. It is easier just to call them by
their names even though we don't understand them
completely. In a similar manner, I prefer simply
to use the term God to refer to the friendly spirit,
the Creator and creating One, my ultimate concern,
the power behind all power, or any other descriptive
term or phrase we may use of God. My perception of
God, like my perception of a friend, is not that
friend, but only a way to help me to organize my
sense data I interpret as coming from that friend,
or from God. When our perception of a friend
proves incorrect, we change our image even though we
use the same name for the same friend. In a similar
manner, our image and understanding of God matures
and can be an aid in our relation with God.

For me, the name "God" refers to the Spirit,
the Creator-Consumator, the Being (or No-Thing)
who stands within and beyond all our experiences.
God is constantly present in the present, yet I
may not be constantly aware of God except as I cognitively remind myself and harken to those 'peak
experiences' or critical meaning-times of amazement
(or "coincidence") when I am especially aware of
God's comfort, support, and leading. Others may call
these times of heightened awareness by other names,
but for me the simple name "God" is sufficient.

As a Christian I point to Jesus the Christ as
the classic expression of God through human life.
The good news is that we don't have to stay in our
self-imposed prisons and shut up in our selfish
"I-castles". This new life is the resurrection, the
new birth, the new city of God which we glimpse
and which we want to happen now in our lives. But
how often we turn our backs on the warm sun and
worship our empty but fearful shadow on the back of

the cave of loneliness and despair. Perhaps our
work in psychology can enable us to discover not
only the reasons that we retreat from real life,
both individually and collectively, but also how we
can move out to create a society of trust, of peace,
of genuine positive affirmation and regard each for
the other. We have a lot of growing to do as we
develop in God's redeeming and creating love.

There are other religious interpretations and
ethical systems among psychologists as there are
among other professions. I ask of any other person
only that she/he act and that each person seek
peace through peaceful means. If the other person
chooses to verbalize about his/her motivations and
world—perspective in ways different from mine, I
welcome him/her. For my part that person is acting
as a person dedicated to God.

Decisions Shape Lives

Religious commitment does make a difference to
a psychologist. My own commitment to God in Christ
enables me to make sense out of each day's events.
My interpretation of God shapes my responses to the
daily tasks of my life. I continue to find that
regardless of how difficult life appears at times,
there is always One to whom we can turn for strength,
courage, wisdom, and clarity of motivation and mind.

It is not whether one believes in God but rather,
by which God one lives. Our tremendous scientific
advances, most of which are yet to come, occur only
because we have learned to listen carefully to God's
creation and discipline ourselves to comprehend
God's work. This basic attitude of trust and humility in the presence of our physical and social
world and the desire to join in the creative process
that will yet bring life from death is the contribution of our faithful (but sometimes not verbalized)
confidence in God.

I probably haven't supplied enough details to
share the richness out of which my life-meanings have
emerged, but you can correct this. Find yourself a
few psychologist Christians (and other types, also)

32

and visit them in their offices. Then you can make
this a more personal exploration. Perhaps you can
discern whether the Word has indeed become flesh
in each person. If you really want to know what we
do, come see us. Perhaps God is calling you to join
us. If so, prepare well. If not, perhaps your calling is to support this type of work in some way.
If so, do it now. If not, then find the way in
which you can maximize your contribution to others
and do it now.

From my perspective, God's gifts of time and
life are inextricably bound together. Out of the
Future the richness of our own lives and the lives
of our loved ones, friends, and other unfold in the
multimedia of time-space that call the Present. As
these meanings and experiences take their places in
the Past, we continually recall them in order to
know ourselves anew as God knows us. Perhaps it is
in this process that we may discover the Presence in
whom we live, move, and have our existence.

Gary R. Collins is Professor of Pastoral Counseling and Psychology at Trinity Evangelical Divinity School. He is a clinical psychologist who has devoted his life to the integration of biblically based Christianity and psychology. Toward this end he has written over twenty books the best known of which are You can profit from stress, How to be a people helper, The Christian psychology of Paul Tournier, and The rebuilding of psychology.

Dr. Collins recently spent a year in Switzerland during which he wrote The Christian psychology of Paul Tournier. He considers that year to be a turning point in his career. Thus, the title of his chapter, Switzerland revisited, is a testimony to that experience. He writes that the year convinced him afresh of the value of Christian counseling and the importance of being a person of integrity.

Dr. Collins lectures widely and is well known among Christian scientists. He recently served a term as president of the American Scientific Affiliation.

Switzerland Revisited
by
Gary R. Collins

"Daddy" the little voice called from the back seat of our blue Opal as we turned on to Route de la Capite and headed toward the French border. "Daddy, will we ever come back to Geneva?"

I was too choked up to answer and so was my wife. In the rear view mirror I could see a little band of our Swiss neighbors who had come to see us off at 6:30 on that Good Friday morning in 1972. The neighbors may not have realized the extent of their influence but my wife and I already were aware that we had just completed what was sure to be one of the most significant periods in our lives.

We really hadn't planned it that way. Our purpose in travelling to Switzerland seven months earlier was simple: to study the life and work of Paul Tournier. I have never been attracted to his rambling style of writing, but I had long been impressed by Tournier as a man who had had the courage and intellectual ability to make such great strides in integrating his Christian faith with his psychology. During my time in graduate school, and subsequently as a college professor and seminary teacher, I had wrestled with this problem of integration. Mostly the wrestling had been done alone for prior to 1970 very few people had written anything of significance in this area - at least from an evangelical perspective. Tournier, I perceived, was one exception. He was known as a competent counselor who was interested not only in Christianity as a religion but in the Bible as the Word of God. I had hoped that exposure to this aging Swiss physician would help me to integrate my psychology with my conservative, biblically based theology.

Initially, Tournier wasn't too enthusiastic about the project. "I shall be very glad to meet you and to speak with you about your ideas and projects," he wrote in my response to my letter asking to work with him, "but I shall not have opportunity to work with you. I am too old and I am not a professor ...For a sabbatical year you need another kind of person than I am". At first I was disappointed, but then decided to go to Switzerland anyway and the subsequent months in Europe proved to be life altering.

Of course there had been other significant events in my life. There was, for example, my conversion, but the details of this are vague in my memory. It occurred when I was very young and heard in Sunday School that all of us sinners in need of a Savior. At a young age, too early for me to remember, I must have committed my life to Christ but, just to be sure, on several subsequent occasions I confessed my sin and invited Christ again to come into my life and control it.

Also significant in my life were the years in college in the Navy Reserve. I had always felt insecure, inadequate and unaccepted by my peers during grade school and teenage years. I wasn't very agile (or interested) when it comes to sports, I didn't attend high school dances because of my religious convictions, and I was only a mediocre student. My greatest acceptance and spiritual direction came from a dynamic church youth group which I attended faithfully. Most of the leaders in the group were two or three years older than I was, however, and it always seemed that they saw me as a kid to be tolerated rather than a friend to be accepted. All of this changed when I enrolled at McMaster University. With a new set of friends I discovered that I was academically more capable than I had ever dared hope. As a freshman I joined the Navy and my subsequent military experience, along with the college classroom, put my faith to the test and proved that Christianity really does work under pressure. These experiences also built my self confidence, and success in the Navy program did wonders to convince me that I really could be masculine, even without athletic prowess. I even debated about becoming a career officer, but withdrew because I didn't like a system where drinking with senior officers seemed to be a prerequisite for promotion. Neither did I like the idea of not being a line officer, preparing

to drive mighty war ships into battle while I
issued orders from the bridge. Because I wore
glasses, they wanted me to be a supply officer-
ordering meats, toilet paper and other equipment for
the daily maintenance of the ship's company. I
wanted none of that so I quit the Navy and decided to
let them fight their wars without me.

My marriage at age 29 was also a significant
turning point in my life - more important even than
getting a hard earned Ph.D. diploma in psychology
several months previously. There was a time when I
felt I'd never find a wife. I don't consider myself
to be especially handsome and I had never allowed
my friendships with women to become serious, lest
this destract me from the goal of completing my
education. I had learned, however, that God is concerned about the smallest details of a Christian's
life and one day I asked Him to give me a wife within
a year or take away my strong desire to get married.
Roughly one year later, on July 18, 1964, Julie and
I exchanged vows. That this attractive, capable
and spiritual woman would be willing to spend her
life with me was not only an answer to prayer, it was
a further boost to my self confidence and created
a great sense of gratitude and wonder which still
persists.

Important as these and other events in my life
have been, however, it was still a sabbatical year,
spent with my wife and daughters in Europe, that I
look upon as the turning point in my professional
life. There were several reasons for this.

First our time in Europe gave me a new appreciation for counseling. In graduate school many
years before, I had concluded that counseling didn't
really work and this view had been reinforced over
the years. In Tournier, however, I saw a successful
counselor. He personified for me what others had
been finding in their research; that the warmth,
genuineness and empathy of the counselor are of
crucial and primary importance in effective people
helping. Tournier was not much interested in techniques, but he was deeply interested in people and
this appeared to be the real reason for his writing

and counseling effectiveness. I was reminded of Gordon Allport's conclusion that "love - incomparably the greatest psychotherapeutic agent - is something that professional psychiatry cannot of itself create, focus, nor release.... By contrast, religion - sepecially the Christian religion - offers an interpretation of life and a rule of life based wholly upon love.... Religion, we conclude, is superior to psychotherapy in the allowance it makes for the affiliative need in human nature."[1] Tournier's life radiated the love of Christ and this, I concluded, was the basis of his counseling success. I determined to change my approach both to counseling and to teaching. In the future, I decided, there would be less focus on technique, but more emphasis on building living, helping relationships.

Secondly, our time in Europe gave me a new view of missions. We had been invited to spend a week in Vienna speaking to American missionaries in Europe, and the experience was, to say the least, enlightening. For the first time I saw some of the dedication, frustration, persistence and stress that face the modern missionary. I determined during that week to apply my psychological skills in the future to the task of helping missionaries and mission organizations with their incredibly difficult but important work.

Third, and perhaps most important, our year abroad gave me a new perspective on my career. Before going overseas my wife had tried without success to convince me that I was becoming a workaholic - driven by conscious and probably unconscious motives to succeed, to write more books, to build the empire of Gary Collins. All of this came to a grinding halt when we arrived in Geneva. For two months we were without books (our trunks had been delayed on a pier in Germany). We didn't have money to travel and for the first (and only) time in memory I literally had nothing to do. Surely this was providential for God used that quiet time to show me the futility of my lifestyle. I got to know my wife and

---

[1]Gordon Allport, The Individual and His Religion (New York: Macmillan, 1950), p. 90, 92,93.

kids again. We took some long walks, had some lengthy
discussions, brushed up on our French, and re-exa-
mined our values and priorities.

Once again Tournier helped without his ever
knowing it. He wasn't a status seeker. He didn't
drive himself or seek publicity. Instead, he wanted
solely to be God's instrument, touching his world at
his pace. I was determined to slow down and to let
God provide the opportunities for my career. No
longer, I decided, do I as a Christian need to fin-
agle, politic, or push myself. It's been a difficult
lession to learn; one which I think is easier to
apply in European cultures than in hard driving
North America. And, I'm still learning: It is God
who "puts down one and exhalts another" (Psalm 75:7).
We have no reason to boast in our accomplishments. If
a gook, counseling session or other project fails,
this can be reason to praise God; if there is success,
this is reason for praise too. I was reminded in
Geneva that my life, family, and career had to be
placed in the hands of God. "No good thing does
He withold from those who walk uprightly", I read
in the Psalms, "How blessed is the man who trusts" in
God (Psalm 84:11-12). We had seen this demonstrated
repeatedly as God provided for us in Europe often
through the love and generosity of our new found
Swiss neighbors. It was a lesson in priorities
that I determined to bring home.

I also wanted to bring back a fourth lesson
from Europe, a new dedication to God. Geneva, of
course, was the home of John Calvin and his influence still persists centuries after his death. I
decided during our Swiss sojourn to read about
Calvin's life and to visit some of the places where
he had worked. One book which impressed me greatly,
more because of it's title than it's contents, was
Jean Cadier's The Man God Mastered. In future years,
I wondered, will anyone ever look at me and say,
"Gary Collins was a man God mastered"? I was determined to become such a man through a new dedication
of my life to Christ and resolve to spend a large
block of time each day (like Tournier does) in
prayer and meditation on the Scriptures. 2 Peter
1"3-11 became my blueprint for action - a model of

what I wanted God to make me: faithful and trusting,
morally pure, knowledgeable, self controlled, patient,
godly, loving - to which I added "a servant, a man
of prayer, one who is familiar with the Scripture,
humble, compassionate, wise, joyful, sensitive to
others, cheerful, authentic and a man who enjoys
life." It was a long list which still I pray about
every day. At first, I naively expected that God
would grant these traits immediately, but shortly
thereafter I took a more realistic perspective after
reading a helpful and insightful quotation by someone named Hugh B. Brown. It is a quotation which has
described my experience over the years. He wrote:

> We ask for strength, and God gives us diffi-
> culties which make us strong.
> We pray for wisdom, and God sends us problems,
> the solution of which develops wisdom.
> We plead for prosperity, and God gives us
> brain and brawn to work.
> We plead for courage, and God gives us dangers
> to overcome.
> We ask for favors, God gives us opportunities.
> This is the answer.[2]

Most men, it appears, have a mid-life crisis
at some time between 35 and 50. I had mine, I believe, in Geneva when I was 38. Before coming home
we spent four months in Cambridge and I returned
with two manuscripts, one completed (The Christian
Psychology of Paul Tournier, Baker, 1973) and the
other in first draft (The Rebuilding of Psychology,
Tyndale House, 1977). But I came home with something
more - a new perspective on my life, faith, priorities, and work; a perspective which has guided much
of my thinking since.

My Work as a Psychologist

A few days after receiving my doctorate from
Purdue University I stood with a friend looking over
the lush green fields of a farm in Western Oregon.
"One thing you will discover," my friend suggested,
"is that professional men rarely find themselves
before age 40."

---

[2]From The Christian Reader, June-July, 1971, p.33.

I could hardly believe what I heard. At the
time I was 28 and 40 seemed like an eternity away.
"How can anyone still be creative and spry at 40?"
I wondered. Twelve years later, on the day that I
turned 40, I gave a little talk to one of my classes
on the fun of being middle aged. "There is no age
I'd rather be, " I told my students, and I really
meant what I said. I had come to realize that my
friend in Oregon had been right.

My work now consists of three major parts,
writing, teaching and speaking - probably in that
order of importance. I also do a lot of counseling,
mostly with students and primarily on a short-term
informal basis, and some time is taken up with administrative work. Others, of course, have different
likes and dislikes, but counseling usually bores
me and administration is challenging only when I
am launching some new program. Committee meetings,
faculty meetings, church business meetings, and
other similar activities are, from my perspective,
time consuming, dull, largely unnecessary, and best
avoided whenever it is possible to do so without
shrinking my dities. My real interest is in writing,
teaching and occasional speaking.

Each of these activities strengthens the others.
My teaching forces me to be relevant, in depth, and
aware of the developments in my field. This makes
me a better speaker and writer. My writing forces
me to relate to people outside of the "ivory tower".
This makes me a more relevant writer and better
teacher. In all of my professional activities, I
have one overarching goal: to integrate psychology
and a biblically based Christianity in theoretical
and practical ways to the end that God's will shall
be accomplished through me and that lives will be
changed.

In all of this work, I start with the assumption that God exists and is the source of all truth.
Much of this truth has been revealed through the
written word of God, the Bible, but truth also comes
through science, experience and the world of scholar-
ship. The competent Christian psychologist, therefore, must have both an in depth knowledge of the

Scriptures and a thorough familiarity with the
developments in his or her field.

I work on the assumption that God's Word, the
Bible, will never contradict God's world as revealed
through science and the arts. Paul Meehl, Lutheran
layman and former president of the American Psych-
logical Association, stated this concisely in a book
which was published several years ago:

> The Christian psychologist...takes it for granted
> that revelation (the Bible) cannot genuinely
> contradict any truth about man or the world
> which is discoverable by other means. If such
> appear to have happened, he must operate on the
> assumption that this is only an appearance.
> That being presupposed, he then seeks to resolve
> the contradiction...If a resolution cannot be
> effected, the problem is put on the shelf as a
> mystery, not solvable by the lights of nature
> or of grace by only in the light of glory.[3]

If for some reason, there must be a decision
between the teaching of Scripture and the conclusions
of psychology, I choose the former, assuming that in
order for there to be truth and stability, all of
our scientific work (including our psychology) must
be tested against Scripture and not vice versa.

Integrating My Faith and My Psychology

My faith enters into every aspect of my work as
a psychologist. _Indirectly_ my beliefs have an influence on my values, my priorities, my decisions,
how I spend my time, what I do during the day and
what I choose not to do. In so far as it is possible
I want to become a man of God (one whom God masters),
a man of balance (whose work, family, worship, and
relaxation all get their due portion of my time), a
man of knowledge (who is familiar both with the
Scriptures and with trends in psychology and tehology),
and a man of compassion (who has a deep concern for
the people in my home, my classes, my neighborhood,
my church and my world). I believe that the committed
Christian cannot divorce his work from his faith. If

---

[3]Paul Meehl, et. al., _What, Then, Is Man?_
(St. Louis: Concordia, 1958), p. 181.

they don't fuse together at least on the level of
values and priorities one isn't very important.

My employment in a theological seminary gives
me an unusual freedom to work at the whole task of
integration. Directly, my faith has a bearing on
my writing, speaking, teaching, counseling, and administrative responsibilities.

Consider, first, the issue of writing and speaking. In his presidential address to the American
Psychological Association, George Miller once suggested that we need to "give psychology away" so that
it becomes helpful and relevant to non-psychologists.
This is one of my goals as a Christian, especially in
an era when believers and non-Christians alike seem
so intent on devouring popular psychology books and
seminars which too oten are created by well-intention-
ed but psychologically naive people.

It is reported that the late Donald Gray Barn-
house once stated that we need, as speakers and
writers, to get the hay out of the loft and down
where the cows can eat it. This is one of my goals -
to make psychology and Christianity clear and helpful to people who have no expertise or familiarity
with the jargon of academia. I believe, however, that
tall animals need to eat too, and I am adventuresome
enough to attempt, on occasion, to write at a higher
more scholarly level. Books like Coping with Christ-
mas or You Can Profit from Stress are geared to the
non-specialist. The Rebuilding of Psychology has
been written for the student or professor who is
more sophisticated psychologically.

Writing and speaking are forms of "public
people helping" which can reach people who otherwise
might never visit a counselor, never hear a preacher,
never get personalized help or never consider how
Christianity and psychology can be integrated. People
who are skeptical of psychologists or afraid of
preachers can also be reached when they read or listen
to a speaker. It's safer to hide in a crowd or read a
book when the author doesn't know you. In communicating, I try to reach people where they are and to
offer practical help - without being bombastic, cynical or simplistic. I believe that psychology can

43

lead us to greater self understanding but I also believe that psychology is incomplete apart from the truths taught in the Bible. I'm not afraid to state these beliefs openly and as often as I can.

Teaching presents a different challenge. My students are about equally divided between seminarians who will be entering the ministry and Christian psychology majors who hope to become counselors. Like me, these people for the most part already are convinced of the authority, relevance, inspiration and inerrancy of Scripture. They need to see, however, how they can apply the truths of the Bible and the finding of psychology to their work as counselors and people helpers.

In my teaching I try to be organized, "up to date" in my subject matter, concise and open to new ideas. I try to model authenticity, spirituality, and sensitivity, and I avoid giving the impression that I have all the answers or that I don't struggle in my personal and spiritual life. If we as teachers pretend to "have it all together" when we don't, we are being phony and encouraging our students to do likewise. Nothing can be more devastating to a ministry or counseling career.

At this point, I might answer a question which comes with some degree of frequency: "Gary, how do you get so much done?" Part of the answer lies, I suspect, in the boundless energy which God has given to me and in the creative mind which is always generating new ideas. In addition, however, there is something which might be called "double duty." In almost all of my activities I try to see how the work in one situation can apply to another. A speech to a convention or Sunday School class, for example, might be worked into class notes and eventually be put into a book. All of my books come out of student discussions and my classes and lectures for the most part have been prepared with books or articles in mind.

In all of this I try to keep alert to research. I encourage students to do empirical research especially as they write their theses and I attempt, whenever possible, to test out my own ideas with experi-

44

ments that yield measurable results. Research is
not a special area of expertise for me, but surely we
as Christians have a responsibility to test out our
ideas and projects before putting them on the market.
Enthusiastic testimonies from sincere church leaders
or laymen may be encouraging, but they hardly prove
that an idea is valid. The more we can test things
empirically and against the Bible (which is what we
tried to do with The People Helper Growthbook) the
less are we guilty of leading people astray with some
program that has face validity but no other proof of
its merit.

Counseling has always been a difficult and less
satisfying part of my work. Within the past few
years, however, I have felt more comfortable in the
counselor's role, primarily because I have relaxed,
become less concerned about proper technique, more
open and willing to share of myself with counselees,
more concerned about building a relationship, freer
in talking about my beliefs, more inclined to suggest
prayer, and less concerned about finding quick solutions to problems which may have taken years to develop.
I have come to see the role of a Christian counselor
as that of a channel through which the Holy Spirit
works to bring healing in another's life. This does
not eliminate a need for the counselor to be skilled
in counseling techniques or familiar with Scripture.
The more we know about counseling and the more we
know about God and His Word the better He can use
us as instruments to touch lives. During counseling,
I often find myself using what one writer has called
"flash prayers" - requests to God for wisdom, insight,
sensitivity, and the thoughts or words which will help
the counseling move in a direction that He desires.

Administration of an academic department,
answering letters, planning seminars, doing committee
work - these are also part of my work, the part
that I don't especially enjoy. I feel, however, that
as a Christian I have a duty to do even these tasks
in as capable a way as I can. God expects His followers to do a good job, even when they are bored, and
I try to comply. To be honest, I also shun like the
plague most invitations to serve on boards and committees.

45

Looking to the Future

It's an established fact in business, I've been
told, that without goals there is rarely any significant progress. The same thing applies to life.
What are the goals for my life, my family, my job,
my writing, my ministry? What are my priorities,
values, plans for the immediate and distant future?
In my opinion these are questions which each of us
should ask frequently.

I have a five year plan for my life, and a
ten year plan. I hope to continue writing, teaching,
speaking and perhaps a little counseling. As funds
become available it is hoped that a Midwest center
can be established for the in depth study of psychology
and theology. I would like to do some further work
in peer counselor training, preventive psychology,
the psychology of missions, pastoral psychology and
the psychology of religion. In each of these areas
I have goals which are specific as well as general;
long range as well as more immediate.

In all of this, however, I have several concerns. First, I am concerned lest I become too
rigid in these plans. Goals are general guidelines
which at times must be revised as circumstances arise.

Second, I am concerned lest I deviate from the
stabilizing influence of the Scriptures. It is not
hard, I feel, to get so caught up in one's psychological work that the Bible becomes less and less
relevant while psychological research or subjective
personal experience become more authoritative.

I am concerned, further, about balance. It
is easy for me to slip into a workaholic lifestyle,
especially easy because I get so many strokes from
admirers who compliment me for getting so much done.
God called me to work, but He also called me to worship, rest, and be both husband and father to my
family.

Fourth, I am concerned about success. To say
I don't want it would be dishonest; to say I'm not
sure I can handle it is more my concern. Success, as
it comes, must be accepted as coming from God. He
permitted it and I pray that He will help me to
cope with it. I trust, furthermore, that I will never
have any followers or disciples. These can be harm-
ful to a man's work and ego, a fact which Jung recognized many years ago when he expressed his gratitude
over the fact that he was Jung and not a Jungian.

There was a time in my life when I so much
wanted to be famous or widely acclaimed that I looked
for chances to push my ministry. Happily, this stage
didn't last long. Today, promoting Gary Collins
doesn't concern me at all. My aim as a Christian
psychologist is to be a man God masters and a man God
uses, as He sees fit, to in some way change the world
in which we live.

III.

THE CRISIS BETWEEN SCIENCE AND RELIGION

Psychologists are scientists. In fact, the
training of psychologists is so full of statistics,
research design, and philosophy of science that
many have decried the loss of the human touch in
psychological education. Nevertheless, psychologists,
like all other scientists, are faced with the
science-religion questions.

. That there are contradictions and problems and
issues between religion and science, cannot be
denied. The psychologists who are also Christians
are faced with these. The two writers in this
section have shared their own dilemmas as well as
their unique solutions.

Both writers have been part of Christian higher
education. Dr. Wiersma teaches psychology at the
undergraduate level while Dr. Vayhinger is a professor in a graduate school. On the one hand, Dr.
Wiersma is concerned with relating his faith to the
questions implicit in the philosophy of science.
On the other hand, Dr. Vayhinger is concerned with
the more traditional questions of how a scientist
can believe in God and participate in acts of personal
piety such as prayer. They illustrate another way
that psychology and faith can be related.

Jack Wiersma is an educational psychologist who has much interest in teacher preparation, a meaningful curriculum, teaching methods and student needs. He is a Professor of Education at Calvin College, Grand Rapids, Michigan.

He has been active as a board member of the Christian Association for Psychological Studies, a national group of persons who are attempting to relate Christianity to the behavioral and social sciences, and is a long time meber of the American Educational Research Association.

A College Professor's "Faithing"
by
Jack Wiersma

What are the dimensions of one's faith pilgrimage? How does one talk about the internalized deposit of one's experience?

In answering these questions, one is, at first, tempted to construe a model that will meaningfully capture those past mental states for which one can cite an approximate date and report significant content. One hesitates at this point for fear of being too analytical. Furthermore, one realizes that these past events not only lack their prior intensity, but have suffered distortion due to the on-going overlays of new experiences. One's heart suddenly goes out to the archeologist who must often not only reconstruct but infer from distorted data, and one clearly identifies with the dilemma implicit in Heizenberg's uncertainty principle. It is for times such as these that a diary would be helpful, and fortunately I have bits of written material to help in this autobiographical report.

Perhaps one can best proceed by suggesting moments of awareness which apparently scored high on one's psychic Richter scale - if one's memory functions are a valid indice. It should be clear, however, that this essay is not the faith pilgrimage; it is rather a report thereof.

Early Childhood and God

No attempt to document my pilgrimage would be complete without suggesting early childhood experiences which exemplified intense confrontation with the Almighty. Little did I doubt that He heard the prayers of His troubled child, and only upon later reflection do I now perceive these experiences as examples of the scriptural concept of "wrestling with God." Furthermore, it is also significant to note that these petitions were not uttered because they might be answered, but rather because they

51

arose out of an existential <u>need</u> to ask them.
That childlike need, arising out of a deep-seated
dependence on God, I have often envied in later
years.

In childhood years I also experienced an extremely "close shave" with death which clearly suggested to me that planning my life in consultation
with God was highly appropriate, since He had seen
fit to spare my life in such a high-risk incident.
If one's beliefs actually do guide and direct specific overt behavior - which I believe they do - these
experiences, I believe, significantly directed my
vocational choice, and influenced my lifestyle in
general.

The Hound of Heaven

To mention the above incidents causes me to
recollect that in late adolescence and early adult-
hood the "<u>Hound of Heaven</u>" became my poem. To deal
with the Almighty was not optional; it was a built-
in necessity. I often envied people who seemed less
burdened by complex religio-philosophical frameworks
and who were apparently more spontaneous and existential in their life-style. This had as one of its
correlates a difficulty in understanding and participating in the "joy" dimension of the Christian life.
It appeared to me - and still does, but in a brighter
context - that to be a disciple of Christ initially
poses more problems than solutions. Perhaps faith
for me was more work than joy. Faith was something
to <u>work</u> <u>out</u> rather than to <u>self-indulge</u> in. I now
see that I had not yet realized what it means to be
<u>free</u> <u>in</u> <u>Christ</u>.

My college experience may perhaps be best conceived of as a period in life where a self-conscious
integrative knowing and faithing experience began.
Being mainly preoccupied with the natural sciences,
but dabbling in philosophy, I devoted a large portion
of my energies to articulating what concepts, such
as antithesis, evolution, creation, provincialism,
parochialism, implied for intellectual pursuits and
Christian action.

52

There was to follow a decade of rather extensive preoccupation with such questions as: How does one integrate faith and learning? How does one make geometry Christian? How does one conceive of the relationship between Biblical and scientific data? Numerous papers im my files testify to the presence of this tension.

Upon reflection, the exploration was very provincial, in that the discussion on these topics in the Christian Reformed community was limited to those authors who were "within" the narrowly defined Reformed community. Thus one never really played with live alternatives, but rather engaged in the rhetoric of "in talk", full of rationalization and low on reason. What now also appears clear to me is that I was asking the wrong kind of questions about the relationship between science and religion with the result that it was impossible to resolve basic issues.

During the college years, a great deal of discussion dealt with the meaning of the antithesis. I believe that this significantly affected my style of thinking. With my having rigidly circumscribed the term "Christian", i.e. reformed people, it became very easy to view other Christian perspectives in a pejorative fashion rather than sympathetically attempting to understand them. Thus my provincialism - bordering on bigotry - was, I think, partially responsible for causing undue tension and conflict when I was exposed to secular frames of reference in post-college experiences. It was further unfortunate in that it caused me to dehumanize people who held a perspective other than mine.

Logical Positivism and Gustav Bergman

After my undergraduate education, I spent one year in graduate study at the University of Iowa. This experience was, I think, instrumental in allowing me to test out my mores and beliefs in a less supportive environment. In retrospect, on the academic level, it allowed for two significant experiences. The first of these was taking a course in the history of psychology from Gustiv Bergman, who represented

53

logical positivism at Iowa. Bergman's course was
high voltage shock treatment. How does one combat
a view point which suggests that religious propo-
sitions are neither true nor false but simply invalid?

In retrospect, there is little doubt that there
was a confrontation of faiths. However, the quality
of my response was to attempt to _defeat_ the enemy at
the propositional level. There was too much anxiety
present to allow me to relax and master Bergman's
frame of reference. Thus I listened only to _defeat_,
not to _master_.

I suspect that the long term effect of the Iowa
experience has been my greater respect for the empirically verifiable (using a scientific frame of reference) and the normative (using a faithing frame of
reference). A colleague of mine recently suggested,
in answering a question dealing with differences
between Christian colleges and state universities,
that at the former, among both students and faculty,
there is perhaps a preoccupation with normative type
questions. This perhaps suggests that, although
normative questions are very necessary, neither of
the above mentioned frames of reference are adequate
in themselves, but must be viewed as complimentary.

The other significant experience at Iowa was
seeing a dynamic College of Education at work.
Educational theory and practice, I concluded, was a
legitimate discipline. My antennae were particularly
sensitive to the vitalizing effect research (engaged
in by the professors) had on their classroom instruc-
tions. It was, I suspect, the reason I decided to
study educational psychology at Iowa after eight
years of teaching at the secondary level.

Modeling - A New Discovery

What I had, however, not understood at this
point in time, and which was to occur eight years
later upon my return to the University, was the
notion of models or paradigms. How one could miss
this dimension of theoretical thought for so long is
difficult to imagine. I shall blame neither myself
nor the institutions responsible for my training.

I had encountered modeling in the natural sciences but for some reason I had not applied it to the social sciences. Theology, and educational theory. Nevertheless, I now feel rather strongly that adequate undergraduate education requires introduction to the notion of modeling (frames of reference) for a satis- factory understanding of human experience.

My eight years of secondary teaching were years of experimentation - my activist phase. It began with high hopes of articulating an integrated faith- learning synthesis, but ended in failure. The integration often seemed superficial with God tacked on to subject matter. Little did I realize that once again my problem was due to a lack of modeling ability. The only paradigm (although I didn't know it was one), which I could (to some degree) articulate was theolo- gical. It is now clear to me that, in order to function as a Christian educator one needs multiple paradigms (theological and non-theological) in order to adequately understand the complexity and diversity of the human experience.

Iowa Revisited

Thus my second Iowa experience for the doctorate, although reacting in rather defensive style to new input the first year, resulted in knowledge and appre- ciation of a variety of paradigms in the behavioral sciences. This led to an awareness of such concepts as process models, intervening variables, and secon- dary and tertiary causation, etc., all of which had the power to add new meaning to what I had experienced as a teacher.

A word must be said about the process of inter- nalization of my beliefs and values. It is my sincere opinion that it is in moments of tension and crisis, that a high probability for the incarnation of the Word in man exists. Thus, it was the doctoral candi- dacy years that may be described as my existentialist phase. At some point there occured an awareness of internalization with an intensity not previously experienced. This is not to suggest that there was no prior internalization of ideas. But this new

55

internalization took place in a context where live
alternative points of view made up the environment and
the internalization was, I believe, more thorough,
more meaningful, and long lasting. But why existentialist phase?

Truth in Me

One of the psychological correlates of such
internalization is the overwhelming feeling that one
no longer needs to defend the Truth; in flesh and
blood one is part of the Truth. The reliance on
objective reality tends to decrease and become rather academic in the light of the inner certainty one
possesses about one's own faithing processes. No
longer is one anxious about meeting the group norm.
In a sense one becomes his own norm. Ideographic
data is one's primary concern. One senses that
significant cognitive and affective content have
become integrated to to form a lasting psychical
deposity. Truth in the abstract is supplanted by
what is "truth for me"; that to which my whole being
can testify. This is that happy moment of higher-
order self-discovery.

At this point in time I see the general model
for my intellectual life as being a tension model.
Tensions develop at the level of rhetoric (ideas
which cause conflict). One can be open to all the
rhetoric, and in fact, in suspension between a number of frameworks at the propositional level. However in the midst of these theoretical alternatives
one must also be in touch with one's own inner
faithing processes if one is to avoid continual
identity crisis. This self-awareness (both cognitive
and affective) is the final basis of appeal and
source of strength. It is God in us and us in God.
It is, I am convinced, some kind of a psychical
residue which is both conscious and unconscious in
composition; it has the qualities of complete internalization in the sense that it represents the core
of the existential self.

My Vocation

Vocationally, I am involved in teacher education as Professor of Educational Psychology at Calvin College. I am first and foremost interested in <u>curriculum theory</u> <u>and</u> <u>development</u> based on a theory of human behavior from a socio-psychological perspective. Within professional teacher education we need more process research regarding the stages of cognitive and affective functioning within teacher education candidates. This data would, I suspect, suggest that we must radically individualize our instructional models in order to achieve meaningful patterns of development in students. The still somewhat worshipped coverage model must give way to a realistic divergent learning model. The end goal is to allow persons to achieve sufficient understanding in order to conceptualize and articulate a wide variety of teaching strategies (paradigms). Unless we achieve this goal through carefully structured learning experiences, our teachers will become either fadists or victims of their own unexamined experience.

I mentioned earlier that my background suggested that certain ecclesiastically controlled or church affiliated academic institutions seem to specialize in asking normative questions. Such a mental set tends to be rather anti-empirical by default. Thus, I perceive it to be part of my responsibility to help with researching what is being done in order to help create a Christian pedagogical science. General revelation must be taken seriously. As a result, no task, if it involves the potential for dealing more appropriately with the created order, is beneath our dignity to research. This usually involves more than stating moral imperatives that must govern our overt behavior in teaching procedures. It must include the collection of all sorts of data which will allow for empirically based day-to-day teaching procedures. Tournier's comment is appropriate, "No religious principle should be based on a faulty psychological framework." Tournier's concept should also apply to situations where pedagogical principles are involved.

Day-to-Day Faithing

With the above perspective, all of life can be
religious in that it assumes that one cannot know the
Truth; according to the Gospel of John, Christians
must do the Truth. One must assume that one's day-
to-day doings vocationally are part of one's faithing.
And if one's inner self has intensely confronted
the Almighty, one must believe that one's faithing
has appropriate guidance. As a self-check, one must
continue to dialogue with the larger professional
Christian community.

SCIENCE AND RELIGION RECONSIDERED

By

John M. Vayhinger

John M. Vayhinger is a United Methodist minister
and a clinical psychologist. He has taught on the
faculties of such institutions as Indiana University,
Garrett Biblical Institute at Northwestern University,
and Iliff School of Theology at the University of
Denver. He is presently Professor of Psychology and
Pastoral Care at Anderson School of Theology, Anderson,
Indiana.
He has been a focal force in relating psychotherapy with Christian theology. He has emphasized
learning therapy as a basis for Christian counseling.
He has lectured and written widely. He is a diplomate
in clinical psychology, the American Board of Pro-
fessional Psychology.

Science and Religion Reconsidered

My History

Perhaps a word of history is in order since one's
views of oneself do not spring full-blown from some
immaculate source but obviously are rooted in one's own
cultural foundations and personal experiences. As an
adolescent and a young man (until half way through
college) I identified with a father, lost when I was
twelve years old, who was a functional agnostic. While
not primarily vocal against religion or belief in God,
he practiced "non-attendance" in religion. Raised in
a deeply religious home (his father was a minister
and a university president, his mother was a social
worker), he came back from World War I with a deep
distruct of verbal idealism. My temperament and my
identification with him left me indifferent to things
of the spirit or religion.

During depression years, my mother held our family
together against terrific odds, making a home where my
younger brother and I unfailingly found security and
encouragement toward independence and education. Late
in my sophomore year of college I was involved in a revival meeting in Cincinnati where the Reverend Charles
Babcock was the evangelist. With several close friends
I went to the altar and was "converted". This 'about-
face' included a change from forestry as a vocation
(saving the forests) to the ministry (saving men).
Reluctantly, almost with regret, I discarded my aspirations to be a conservationist "in nature", to be a
"pastor" with people. As I worked through, intellectually, what this profound experience meant, I felt
clearly that my calling was to become a teacher in the
conserving and educating function of the ministry, to
teach counseling and pastoral care in a seminary. This
deep sense of calling has never left me, and today,
nearly thirty-five years after the experience, the
direction is as clear and strong as it was in that college dormitory room.

So in the years following, I completed college,
spent three years in seminary, obtained a master's degree in philosophy, studied two more years for a
master's degree in experimental-abnormal psychology,

and then took a doctorate in clinical psychology.
Earlier, I had planned on a medical degree also, feeling the necessity of understanding "the whole men", but
experience led me to decide against it as unnecessary
for my calling. While a student at Columbia University, the College of Physicians and Surgeons was kind
enough to allow me to take some basic courses in medicine in the areas of anatomy, physiology, and central
nervous system functioning.

Recognizing also the necessity of clinical involvement, I spent thirteen years as a pastor or as a
minister of pastoral counseling, and seven years as the
chief clinical psychologist in a psychiatric clinic.
Seven years were spent in teaching undergraduate
psychology in a church college and a state university.
Some of these years overlapped with the clinic position. Then a call came for me to go to a Methodist
Seminary as a research professor in pastoral psychology
psychology of religion and pastoral care in the seminary.
For nearly fifteen years I have nad a small private
practice and a number of consulting relationships in
industry, pastoral clinics and psychiatric centers, as
well as with a number of church bodies and clerical
groups.

My Assumptions

From these experiences have come a number of concerns. When I was still in school, I became acutely
conscious of the fundamentalist-liberal, conservative-
modernist conflicts in the church, and determined I
would not be hung up on these polarizations. I quite
consciously chose both a conservative and a liberal
seminary and spent two years in each. It seemed such
a tragedy that people of good will, serving the One
God, would band together in partisan groups.

In everyday decisions I have been a functional
skeptic, though questioning, not doubting. Even as
I decided to attend both a conservative and a liberal
seminary in order to gain a broad spectrum of theological information and attitude, so I selected a
graduate school of psychology within which I could
be exposed to psychoanalytic, humanistic and behavioral types of training.

Introduction to theological 'myths' formed a
fine basis for scientific and psychological 'myths'.
This does not indeed belittle the "truths" in these

61

psychological and theological frameworks, but it does
enable one to read Freud and Rogers and Skinner and
find important information in each, or to believe
sincerely in a theological Person who is revealed in
the Bible and to understand (at least to some degree)
what the theologian means when he/she speaks of eternal life and sin and salvation and holiness.

I have always found relative amounts of tension
between my religious faith and my scientific commitments, but never contradiction or conflict. And always I am amazed at the vast amount of "faith" most
scientists have to have to be scientists: It takes
real faith to believe that the senses and their ex-
tensions in tools and measuring devices are accurate,
and that natural law is continuous in space and time.

I have learned patience for the profound questions in both science and theology. Reality is so
vast--time is short--and experience is complex. For
instance, when I first became a Christian, I enter-
tained (along with a kind of uncritical humanism)
beliefs in persons' ability to perfect themselves and
their society, given the information usable by their
intelligence. Then in reading Freud, I discovered an
explanation for persons' deeply-rooted characteristics
of hostility, destructiveness and illogical pain-giv-
ing, which I had observed many times. This was at
variance with my humanistic views. Freud's clinical
descriptions, though lacking vital elements of what
we would today call a case history, were fresh and
insightful--and suddenly I saw what the theologians
termed "original depravity" or "original sin". Some
of the descriptions even fit Freud's own moodiness
and suspicion of his own disciples. It is a profound
unconscious tendency to react destructively to oneself and to others. I have seen many persons in
psychotherapy unconsciously respond to the opportunity
for a better self-regard or more meaningful relationship with a significant person, by seemingly
"deliberately" sabotaging the situation. And I understood what St. Paul meant when he said "I have the
will to do good, but not the power. That is I don't
accomplish the good I set out to do, and the evil I
don't really want to do I find I am always doing."
(Romans 7:19-20, Phillips).

There are, of course, profound questions left
still. Theology and Freud would assign differing
causal agents to man's fall from grace versis

62

infantile residues and childhood trauma to the condition, and each would have differing techniques for relieving the condition. Freud would recommend free-association and interpretation, while theology would advise repentance, restitution and faith.

Another issue is "guilt" which is almost always seen by the Freudians as "guilt-feeling, i.e. a psychological state or condition where one feels a sense of doing wrong or inability to measure up to his own ideal self or someone's goal for him/her. To the theologian, on the other hand, guilt refers to an objective ethical or forensic relationship between person and person, or between person and God. It is thus a condition which is to be solved, not a feeling to be resolved. As Jeeves describes them, "not only is it not the same thing to feel guilty and to be guilty, but the two do not even necessarily exist in direct proportion. When these two different meanings of the word 'guilt' are confused, needless and groundless conflict is invariably generated."[1] The psychologist Christian, being aware of "feeling" and "being" as differing, is able to distinguish appropriately the situation and the therapeutic needs of the patient or the sinful person. Clinically, to be sure, both are nearly always present in the same patient, though one or the other predominates in the clinical symptoms. I have tried to avoid reducing theology to psychology, or vice versa.

Being a Christian: Does it Make a Difference?

I have often asked myself, "Where does my being a Christian make a difference in my psychology?" Certainly not in my skills, for my training in research methodology, in psychodiagnosis and psychotherapy, are essentially the same as that of most experimental and clinical psychologists. Is it in my openness to persons, ability to listen to what they mean in their hurt and suffering and conflict? Maybe a little, for the religiously sophisticated therapist may listen to a broader spectrum of meaning in a person's affective suffering than one who is secular and agnostic. At least there is less likelihood of ignoring or rejecting the authentic religious conflict or anxiety. Certainly it is not in honest concern for persons, for every psychologist hopefully is open and interested in

[1] Jeeves, Malcolm A. The Scientific Enterprise and Christian Faith. Intervarsity Press, 1969, p.121.

those persons for whome he/she has responsibility.
Perhaps, in part at least, it is in a broader and
deeper empathy with the spiritually conflicted person.
And certainly there is a difference when working with
or studying persons who are seeking a religious orientation to life (either as professional religious
leaders or simply as individuals who have made an
authentic choice for religion). Here, a therapist
with a religious experience would have resources and
skills and insights beyond those of the secular psychologist. At least, I believe it to be so.

Here is the essential difference between the non-
Christian psychologist who only observes persons who
hold the "conviction that there exists a paternal
deity, omniscient and omnipotent, with whom the individual is able to communicate (for example, through
prayer or sacrament) and by whom he/she feels personally known and loved."[2] and the psychologist who can
pray, "Our Father who are in heaven."

Specific Concerns for the Psychologist Christian

Many observable human experiences provide tension, not so much in their doing, as in their explanation. For the religious person, prayer and choice and
symbols are all believable experiences. In the psychologist, searching for cause-effect relationships, they
may seem something quite different.

First, let's take prayer, William Adams Brown
testifies to his conviction that:

> If God, to be Creator, purposing as well as
> acting, prayer becomes a most reasonable ex-
> ercise, for prayer is that form of human
> experience in which man, the person, communes
> with the personal God.[3]

I have only to say, an explanation is beyond our
contemporary explanations, but within our immediate
participation for conclusions. I do it consistently
and, like digestion, supersonic travel psycho-

[2]Gill, James J. The Psychology of Religious Development. In E. Mansel Pattison (Ed.) Clinical Psychiar-
tic Clinics, Vol. 5, no.4, 1969.

[3]Brown, William A. The Life of Prayer in a World of
Science, Scribners, 1927, p.36

therapeutic healing and human conception, I do participate joyfully in trust and faith rather than in logic
and analysis.

Here are some of my prayers where I find, in my
work, a complimentarity between my faith and its theological expression and my skills in clinical psychology. There seems to be no conflict, though tension
is often a part of their co-existence, even in their
compliemtarity. I am asked, "do you pray in therapy?"
My answer is always, "Yes, of course. All the time.
Like this, though not out loud:

> Help me to be sensitive, Father, and alert,
> to be able to hear what my patient is say-
> ing, on so many differing levels and in so
> many different languages. Open my senses
> and my experiences, along with my skills.
> May I know what my friend is meaning, may I
> listen to what he/she is thinking and may I
> understand what he/she is communicating.
> Keep me, Lord from magical thinking, or from
> placing my trust in mechanical and determin-
> istic theory, or from closing my thinking
> with only some of my patient's facts. But
> most of all, Holy Spirit, come as Counselor
> that I may share my humanity with this suffer-
> ing person in order that we may together find
> peace and direction in this community. In
> Christ's name I ask this. Amen.

Or when doing research:

> Make me aware, Creator of this universe, of
> my biases; and to compensate for these in my
> design. Alert me to prejudices and eliminate
> them from my research as I attempt to discover
> the laws of Thy universe. Help me to evaluate
> the data, to measure the samples, to form con-
> clusions that are valid and accurate and to
> truly love, in peace and justice, those who
> have made this society with their blood and
> tears and successes. May I learn by their
> failures and build upon their gains. Give my
> programmer logical analysis, my graduate
> students accuracy in their data collection and
> copying, my correlations significance, and my-
> self humility in interpreting my conclusions.
> Create in me patience that I not conclude my

experiment before enough data is in, and
help me to be strong enough to tolerate
the ambiguity of the decisions I must make
-- for the sake of my human responsibility
and the welfare of all mankind, my brothers
and sisters and Your children. Amen.

Or when in social involvement:

When need is great and my resources and
patience are small, Lord, teach me in
affection and concern to love my brother
and sister simply because they are my
brother and my sister. Keep me from reverse
prejudice and racism, and teach me my humanity that I may be humble when I persuade my
brothers and sisters of differing persuasion
to be like me in my understanding--that I
may not be the blind leading the blind into
the ditch of despair. Amd may my work lift
mankind toward the higher brotherhood by their
own choices. For I ask these things in the
Name of One Who made it all in the beginning.
Amen.

Second, I find a necessity to distinguish doubt
from questioning. Just as the relationship of the
physician and patient is first founded on trust, then
faith, so my relationship both with this present world
and with God is founded on curiosity, but not doubt.
Granted that many use the word "Doubt" as "asking
questions about", I would rather see "doubt" confined
to "not believing" or "lack of belief or sureness". I
use "questioning" to refer to what the scientist does
about every law, principle, classification and research
result, as well as what the Christian does as the growing edge of experience and belief.

"To question" would be like a fact or interpretation to be investigated, talked over, considered. On
ultimate concepts, I prefer "question" to "doubt".
The same would prevail on questions of much theological information, such as "eternal life", "the
divinity of Christ", or "the resurrection of Jesus".
Question, then, carries the implication of a positive belief on which one needs more and better information.

"Faith" is the reverse side of "questioning".
Both are necessary for a science and religion. This
faith I see as compounded of at least two elements--

facts upon which logic and reason are based, and trust which depends on experience. These are complementary, not contradictory, except in details. As St. Augustine wrote, "The whole practical life of man is founded on faith.

Scientists and religionists are aware that their knowledge is built upon faith, evolved from experience. Possibly this begins with the belief in the authority or reliability of believable persons in one's life without proof of person experience. One can, indeed, know in one's faith as well as through personal experience, for to know something is to perceive it with certainty and to understand it clearly. Psychological skills help in "asking the questions" about religious information, but they are misused when they promote "doubts" about religious faith.

Lastly, let us consider models and analogies. As I see the task of both psychologists and Christians, it is primarily to learn more and more about "the deeper truth of reality", and to apply what is discovered to the use and benefit of persons. Both must use pictures, images, models, stories, and even parables in attempts to depict reality--and both must be equally careful not to identify their models with what reality really is. Science makes extensive use of concepts like reflex arcs, tenes, electrons, nerve nets, neural traces, ego-id-superego, goal gradient, drive, need, waves, species, and so on. All are useful,but none identify "real things". All are just concepts to describe what we see in the world as it is. Both science and theology would be the poorer, perhaps more impotent, if models and analogies were "demythologized."

So, the scientist in me is sad when some comtemporary theologians want to "demythologize" the traditional language in which God has revealed, and man has discovered, His activity in the world of today. Models such as the Prodigal Son, the Good Samaritan, the miracles of the loaves, and the healing of the blind man, all represent "God in action; as much as an atomic model or DNA represents "reality".

And so, it is rather in the model of the world as regular and its realities as contingent (i.e. needing to be looked for, since they cannot be predicted a priori) that I find my faith in the Christian docttrine of creation and the effectiveness of the

67

scientific method to be fully compatible.

Further, there are times when the Christian must simply determine to believe and behave as a Christian. While understanding the data of behavioral science, and even while participating in research which re- quires an "objective" view of persons as "objects", there comes a time when mental (as contrasted with spiritual) reservations become necessary to the deter- ministic philosophy of behavior. Perhaps it is a re- cognition that while persons behave on one level "as if" they were animals, and on another level "as if" they were machines, and on another level "as if" they were biological organisms, they also behave on an- other level "as if" they were spiritual human beings, children of God, brothers and sisters of all other brothers and sisters, citizens of "two worlds".

Carl Rogers expresses this (though without the theistic implication specified) when, after exploring the mechanistic and controlling trends in the be- havioral sciences, declares his belief in a paradox which does not deny "the objective mechanical view, but which exists as co-equal with it, and this is that man "can never live as an object. He can only live sub- jectively". He continues, "We cannot without great peril, deny this subjective element in ourselves . . . no present or future development of the behavioral sciences should be permitted to contradict this basic fact".[4]

The tension consists in holding a lawful, predic- table model of the world as a base for research and including the belief that persons can and must make choices and choose between alternatives.

In Conclusion

To live as a Christian and as a psychologist is exciting and productive. Tensions occur between inter- pretations of theologically specific data and psycho- logical information. None are irreconcilable, most are minor, even the large ones discussed here are tolerable. Just as science and its practioners believe in the interaction between experience and interpretation so theology and its practioners believe likewise.

I trust that I can always maintain that Christian position position, as a psychologist, just midway be- tween skepticism and credulity in dealing with all

reality realistically. This is what it means to me
to be a psychologist-Christian.

4
 Rogers, Carl R. A Humanistic Conception of Man.
 In Richard Farson (Ed.) Science and Human Affairs,
 Science and Behavior Books, 1965, p. 29.

RELIGIOUS EXPERIENCE: ITS OCCURRENCE AND ITS STUDY

Throughout history the one event that has convinced skeptics of the reality of God has been personal experience. Nothing substitutes for it. Nothing compares with the conviction it brings. Scientists who are religious are often persons who have experienced God in unmistakable events. Their experience often does not fit neatly into their scientific categories. Yet it stands alongside the evidence from their experiments as legitimate and valid.

Drs. Travis, Clark, and Meadow who write in the section are convinced of the reality of the unseen. Dr. Travis, while reared in a Christian family, had not been inside a church for over forty years prior to the life changing experience about which he writes. Dr. Clark, while gently nurtured through all his years in a firm faith, became reconvinced of the power of the "nonrational" in research which focused on triggers of religious experience. He is firmly convinced that modern man steels himself against deeper experiences through an overemphasis on technology and rationality. Dr. Meadow has been haunted by the memory of the presence of God as she has sought to find meaning and purpose for her life. She writes poignantly of alternating fertile and dry periods in her search. Yet, she maintains that her pilgrimage has not been in vain.

These psychologists illustrate the continuing power of religious experience in the lives of persons. For them, it is a power which they cannot deny and which provides the focus of their existence.

Lee Edward Travis is Distinguished Professor and
Dean Emeritus of the Graduate School of Psychology of
Fuller Theological Seminary. Prior to his sojourn at
Fuller, he was professor and head of the Departments
of Psychology at the University of Iowa and of Speech
Pathology at the University of Southern California.
At one point he was listed as one of the top twenty
of the most quoted psychologists in America. He has
chaired over two hundred doctoral dissertations and
is a diplomate in clinical psychology, the American
Board of Professional Psychology. Shortly after re-
tiring from the University of Southern California
when he was in private practice in Beverly Hills, he
had a religious experience in a local Presbyterian
Church. He then became a Christian Psychologist.

IV.

RELIGIOUS EXPERIENCE: ITS OCCURRENCE AND ITS STUDY
by
Lee Edward Travis

In the Spring of 1961 when I was sixty-five and practicing psychotherapy in Beverly Hills, Mrs. Travis and I attended a Sunday morning church service. That was the first time I had gone to church in over forty years.

The sectuary was completely filled. We sat outside in the warm sun listening to the service through a public address system. I have never remembered in either specific or general terms the thrust of the sermon. We didn't see the minister during the service but stood in line at the close to greet him. Although I was affected in an amazing way by the worship experience, I did not tell him anything at all about my feelings.

The Second Week's Experience

A week later we went back to the church, earlier than before, and sat inside where we could see as well as hear. This time I was overwhelmed with emotion and attending physical reactions. I didn't ask immediately what exactly was occurring. I felt only that it was something of great consequence, and that I would have to accept it and live with it as me. I felt I need not ask the meaning, just now anyway, of what was happening; or question the role of the minister about his part in my intense, but not unpleasant disturbance.

The experience of out-of-mindedness did not entirely eliminate the conscious consideration of my situation. The reality of my senses still existed and I could think and reason. Could people see? Could they hear? Whom could I trust? Were I really as sound of mind as I had always thought? Was anyone else affected? Was I the only one in this physical and emotional state and what might I be revealing? Tears, heavy breathing, sobs, groans, what? My wife was beside me but I could get no answers from her. She seemed as well poised as ever. Whether anyone else knew it or not, I was in a state of ecstacy.

73

At first I was only physically present when the phenomenon of transcendence began. Soon, however, I occupied a position of complete absorption in the on-going event. I was not a detached technologist, a manipulator of an event full of facts. Since I did not know what I might experience, I chose observing and living in relation to what was happening with me. I could sense (but not perceive) the nature of the force acting within me. I took the road of wonder over the road of analysis or abstraction. Unhampered freedom flowed between me as object and me as subject. I was not only living, but also I was being lived. I both predated and transcended my current social self. I seemed to have left the congregation to assume the responsibility and burden of being a person.

This had its pain, this loss of identity with outer collectives. I was a singular person, but feeling more passive than active; more as though I were serving as the consequence of an effect solely triggered by an outside agent. There were no threats of bad side-effects immediate or remote from this powerful usurpation of my life by the outside force. Only good results seemed to be present and indicated for the future. All was well, very well indeed.

Living became precious, compelling and devoid of errors. Whatever was, was right. I was caught up in an incredible and impossible way that led beyond my individuality. My sensations extended endlessly and I felt inarticulate. This just could not happen to me, certainly not at this time and in this social context. How ridiculous could this all be? I was a man of strong will-power and clear language, so I thought, I had hold of myself well at all times. This didn't make sense. It was out of all proportion to the stimulus. The environmental situation was a quiet, dignified religious service. Those in attendance were of the upper middle class. They were thoughtful and dignified and respectful of the service and of each other.

This young minister, Dr. Louis H. Evans, Jr., was populat (not especially for his oratory and evangelistic zeal) but mainly for his ability to provoke thought and arouse interest in important social and

74

personal issues. To me his preaching was more a spur
to thought than to action. He could be considered the
intellectual type rather than the persuasive kind of
preacher. All of this is not to say that he was in-
effectual. On the contrary, he was very effective in
his ministerial effort. But never, not at the time
or since, have I felt manipulated by anyone or anything in the church. I was not told how to feel and
there were no models anywhere around for me to follow.
No one else gave any observable signs whatever of
having feelings like mine. And never since then have
I learned of anyone in the church having a transcendental experience at that time or at any subsequent
time. Dr. Evans had no knowledge or feeling that
anything unusual had happened to anyone in the congregation. He did not know me, and had not made any
note of my presence at either one of the two services.

Two experiences - One Week Apart

The two experiences of a week apart were qualita-
tively the same, but they differed in that the second
one was incomparably more intense and encompassing.
To describe it is to include the first. While participating in the service, listening to the prayers and
songs and following the minister's sermon, I floated
in and out of a rich and turbulent internal world of
feelings and sensations. I could not breath. My breath
would not come. It had gone astray; it had been taken
away. Was I dying, or was I dead already? I observed
my body in which I found myself incarnated. I was not
frightened by its loose hold on me, and I felt that I
could go on and on from world to world. The urgency
that shook my body was known intuitively to be completely trustworthy. Still I sensed a new act of
creation in which there was no conformity. Paradoxically, I had no feeling of weakness or of losing consciousness. But still, in some sense I had died and
returned anew.

There was the physiological event of faltering
respiration; the psychological event of utter depen-
dency and helplessness; the social event of the church
services; and the transcendental event of a unitive
bond with Being Itself. I did not focus on any one
of these levels of the experience. I considered it a
single, new event. I was left with no feeling of
exhaustion or weakness, but rather with a sense of

75

transformation. This latter feeling carried in turn,
feelings of surrender, gratefulness for my life, and
unselfish love for others. I felt a sobbing gladness
that life would win; that it would not end. It has
always been here and it would always remain. Death
was out of mode, never winning the final struggle.

I was filled with infinite compassion punctuated
with the wonder of worshipfulness. I would observe,
understand and identify in order that I might forgive
and serve. I experienced a shift from the view that
I must save my own life at all costs to the view that
I must love it, certainly at first, to save it at all.
Only in another life could I live my own. Gone was
any sense of independent existence.

Still, paradoxically, never before had I experienced such heightened self-awareness. I was crystal
clear to myself, yet completely dispersed. I was here,
and everywhere else, simultaneously. At once there
was both an amplification and a diminution of individuality. I was alone, and yet with all else. I could
not name my condition, but only enjoy it.

For what was I searching?

Was I searching for meaning, for the significance
of my living? Was I searching, or was I being search-
ed. Or were both occurring in a condition of complemen-
tarity? I did not ask these questions then for I did
not feel any need for answers. My living had not in
the smallest detail been without continuity. One day
followed another in natural, sequential order, living
was lawful and ordered. And then it came about, a
seemingly sudden event within this natural order.
The natural order was temporarily dissolved and the
occurrence was placed outside of it. By definition,
a miracle had occurred, a discontinuity in the scheme
of things. There was magic and myth now in the living
of my life.

The sun did not stand still. Neither did the
earth open up. Nothing was to be seen or heard to be
reported. I had to be reasonably sophisticated to
perceive the miracle imbedded in the natural. I felt
the chaos of the disruption of the natural order.
And I wondered if there were really any order, or

76

quality of exploiting a troubled soul, of vitiating
free choice, or of precipitating emotionally traumatic
experiences. Instead, my experience partook of me being found out, of me being discovered in my innermost
parts, of a gift of love, or a reconciliation within
and with the whole of creation.

A state of grace

All that was happening was completely effortless
and unmerited by deeds. I was in a state of grace. Was
it something not to be gained by seeking, however
earnestly?   I had long since forsaken religion and the
"church", and I had not the slightest intention to find
either one of them again. They were blocks to be removed even though my experience happened in a church.
I was not on any conscious quest for God or for anything else that I could tell. Rather, the experience
has set me on a quest - a quest to explain or determine
what had happened. And from the beginning I knew
there was no ending to this quest.

Unheard and unseen forces stalked through this
dream-like state of consciousness.   In it I reached
timidly out into the darkness behind me and into the
light around me.   I left the Eden of the eternal present belonging to my senses and rode the winds of my
transcendental existence. Yet I trembled in embarking
upon a quest for the new revelation. The voyage might
carry me into a strange virgin country where I could
risk an irretrievable loss of faith. But the hazard
had been invited because a faith that is not open to
loss is no faith at all. As I glimpsed the way, it
was the metamorphosis of the sacred into the profane.
A way that had no reverse lane to the past, but only
a one-way road ahead.

Questions to be Asked

No miracle can stand telling. It would be no
miracle if it could. I must seek, then, to tell a
natural revelation that will not necessarily suffer
obliteration or even distortion in the sharing of it.
I had not set up a controlled experiment. I was not
confined within the four walls of the laboratory.
Still, I had not fled, into a personalized religion.
Regardless of how or why it happened, I was merely to
be present when the natural (or super-natural) revealed itself most completely. Consciously I had not
anticipated anything particular in going to church.

Simply I felt a mild curiosity about the structure and
its uses up there on top of the mountain above our
home. Was it all by chance; an inconceivable series of
events; the day, the place, the people, the far-away
time out of my past? Did they all combine to furnish
an episode of singular occurrence, never again to re-
appear? Was I an intruder as well as, or instead of,
a participant in the event of that day? Or was I an
observer acting as such in the objective consideration of me in that little individual moment in the
whole of living? Was there a dim, tangible forgotten
thread here joining me with my roots and with my destiny? Was I passing judgment, of life against death,
as though some evil thing were being forgotten? Was
the whole episode, experience, miracle, conversion,
or whatever, a song to the sweetness and beauty of
life? Or was I being sung by all that is or ever was?
When Monday came, would I doubt the meaning of what
occurred and the judgment that it rendered? Would I
remember only the sense of bigness beyond my power to
grasp and portray? Shouldn't I settle for the re-
cording of the event and not strive to define its
significance?

I was impelled with the disquieting feeling that,
at whatever cost, I must not return to "normalcy" to
the specifiables of living. Rather, I must remain in
the vortex of the storm of unspecifiables to risk the
currently unstructured. I felt I must not wait either
until my professional responsibilities had been discharged but stride out now in the quest for an ever-
expanding personal fulfillment. I must seek the inner
way. I must face myself nakedly as a wanderer in the
inner world. Would I find the murky wet, the great
fire, the strong wind, the intense light? I would
know.

Over and over and over again, I have wondered if
the whole experience and the changes that followed
were created out of my own psychological substance.
Did something slumber in me for nearly half a century to be awakened by an apparently gentle nudge?
The awakening, in contrast to the stimulus; was ex-
plosive. My arousal was sudden and shattering. Was
there some particular ingredient in the substance of
my mind that emerged under some command? was some
chord in my psyche unwittingly plucked by the minister? Or was it just a lonely experience resting upon
the invisible and the silent?

78

Surrender and Gratefulness

My problem in the experience was not to deal with
external reality itself. The essential external stimulus was a thoughtful man saying reasonable and seemingly unemotional things in a quiet religious service.
I did not become fearful or guilty but I certainly
did become relatively completely chaotic in the move-
ments of respiration. Both inspiration and expiration
seemed suspended. Yet there was no feelings of faint-
ing or of paralysis. My organic sensations were not
at all unpleasant or threatening. Actually, tears of
joy flowed freely. Deep within my body were pervasive
feelings of complete surrender to the sublime and of
an intense gratefulness for life. Both feelings served
an unselfish love of great power,

Writing, research, and teaching had not been
enough. What these might leave for eternity was of
questionable value. The very most that I could expect
was continued living through the minds of others. So,
too, was it with my children? I could live on in their
minds and bodies. But where was I in these ways of
gaining immortality? Where was my guarantee of everlasting personal continuity with life? Must I have
had a hunger for more than I had and I went in search
of its satisfaction?

No Serious Problem

I have said that I was not facing any serious problems in living. I was in good health and relatively
successful. I was honored personally and professionallly.
My family was a compliment to my role as a father. My
anxiety over world conditions was comparatively low.
True, I sensed an apocalyptic mood dwelling in the
lives of almost everyone and I was affected by it. But
I was not interested in becoming an activist in poli-
tics or social affairs. I felt deeply about injustices
of all kinds and I wrestled mightily with the problem
of evil men. In spite of serving well in both world
wars I have always felt the utter absurdity of mobilizing brains and conscience on the largest scale for
destruction instead of for dealing with man's greatest
needs in living. So what was my problem, if problems
there must be, leading up to that first sunday morning
in the church?

79

In retrospection, these questions seem apt. Very
shortly after the church experience I wrote the following poem:

Save me for you, spare me for your purposes
May I live more, ninety and nine years more
Only for you may I live ninety and nine years

more

You need not spare me just for me
You need not spare me from pain and
suffering

Or from sorrow and hurt and the discouragement
of failure

But please spare me for ninety and nine years
more
To witness to the men of my lengthened life
As only an extraordinarily lengthened life
can witness
In a world of incredulity and utter scorn
In a world of sure prediction and no surprises
In a world of meaningless clock-like momentum
Grinding inexorably the finest atoms into
nothingness

Let me witness to thy purposes
Striding ever far behind in your everlasting
footsteps
Yet striding in ever strengthened faith and
clearer hopes
Declaring unflinchingly the truth of your presence
A truth so clear for all to see who will pause
to see
Needing strongly the sheer living physical witness
Of this truth
Living more, living ninety and nine years more
I will be this vital witness of this truth
I will be the limitlessly open truth abounding
for all to see
My older companions of contemporary doubt and
customary futility
Playing a faceless role of their own selfish making
For them, give me life to serve you, just to
serve you
Not at all in any way, just to serve me
Always in all ways just to serve you
To serve you.

Have I asked too much, am I too presumptuous to
                    ask at all?
Already you have walked with me and have talked
                    with me
Ought I to be sufficiently grateful to accept
                    my short life?
Just for me I would not ask for anything more
                    than my short life
But for you I would ask even for an extension of
                    my short life
To live ninety and nine years more in the witness-
                    ing of your will be done
Upon this earth, this contemporary world of
                    unconcern for you

I would ask your favor and your forgiveness
Bless me oh Lord, for your sake
                    Bless me, oh Lord

Answers to my Questions

The answers to these questions could be that I had
my experience in order to handle an ever-increasing
threat to the continuity of my life. I had relatively
unconsciously grown increasingly sensitive to the
apocalyptic vision of our time. I will repeat again
that I had never been more free from trouble and anxiety, or had more zest for living, than on those two
days in the church. I had no conscious tension over
my death or that of anyone close to me. Both in abstraction and in mild affect I have discerned from my
earliest days of self-reflective consciousness, the
feeling that death was in my birth and also have discerned a wrestling with the disquietude accompanying
this feeling.

As a child I had recurrent night dreams of many
soldiers marching along a broad front intent upon des-
troying me. They were fierce and fully bent upon
their mission. In my agonizing fear for my life and
facing the utter hopelessness of escape to save it, I
joined them. I united with them as fellow human beings.
I became one of them in loving comradeship. We became
citizens together of the human race and smiled warmly
in our acknowledgement of each belonging to the other.

Seemingly as a Child faced with death I could
settle for a trustworthy relation with other human
beings, but possibly, as a man late in life, I would
need to settle only with a companionship with the
infinite. Other people would die and therefore could
not be trusted. Neither was the earth itself trustworthy with its limited supply of life-giving stuff.
My trust must be placed in an inexhaustible source of
self-reflective consciousness. I must have endless
self-awareness. My task would be to extend my uniqueness to completeness in a unitive experience with the
divine. My demand must be that always I would know
that I knew. I must have the grace to confront and
transcend death in a form of resurrection in this life.
The way to meet my demand and need for immortality
came as a revelation on those two Sunday mornings.

A Sense of Immortality

A complete shedding of my separate existence
occurred. In its place came a mentality permeating and
illuminating my senses. I was overwhelmed with the
discovery that I was not self-containing but channels
of the life and energies of the universe. I was freed
from fetters of gravity and substance and became per-
meable to all else. I felt the essence of being, the
billowy translucense of infinite expansion in time and
space. I moved about effortlessly with seeming
weightlessness in a sea of air. I was freed of the
material-binding specifics of perception in a mode of
self-emptying, opening wide to the reception of the
eternal. I had a feeling not compounded of the common
feelings and thoughts of my living, but rather of transcending all mindful operations of experience directly
my unique position in the universe, my spiritual in-
destructability and my timeless existence. I lived
from the beginning, not arising out of some already existing substance. I had always been and I would
always be. I was a particular of all-pervasive living
without beginning and ending. The end of my substance
had arrived and I became boundless and endless in my
being.

For this revelatory experience I will never need
an apology or a justification. Feelings of gratitude
and all-embracing love for everybody and everything
lead me into paths of doing good for the world and into repaying always the indebtedness for the gift of my
everlasting life. To preserve this gift I will live
it in an inexhaustible supply of love, truth, freedom
and encounter.   82

I have been saturated with the essence of being.
I know who I am and I do not need another person to
define me. But I can be with another, even to be he,
because knowing me so well, I can know him also. I
always was and I always will be. I can love you even
without your love in return. But I can accept your
love if you should give it and know that it is helpful.
I have been loved into being and I am continuously
being loved into being. I am freed rather than annull-
ed by the forces of physical and social existence.
Old discrepancies of being alienated and adrift have
been replaced by newly tapped and never before experienced resources.

From Then to Now

The shift occurred radically in the church several
years ago, but has continued and developed more quietly ever since. Absurdities have given way to the discovery of values and meaning in the experience of
transcendence. A reverential awe has ascended to the
throne of self-hood. It fosters a quest for the con-
templative, the observational and the worshipful solution rather than the manipulative, the controlling and
the unsettling. But I remain in the world, if not of
it. I move away from socially supporting and publici-
cally given meaning. Yet I am not alone, either. I
accept the severe pain of man's evil as a sign and a
seal of a deep bond with being itself. I have struck
a regenerative and new stance over the hostile enorm-
ity of despair and anguish. I accept as a given my
never ceasing purpose to be more than I am, to transcend the limits of human understanding and to see
beyond the seemingly prescribed existential limits of
communal living. I will live in a punctured finitude
to wander out into the infinite.

Most important to me was that this experience prepared me to accept the offer to become Dean of the
Graduate School of Psychology of Fuller Theological
Seminary. Looking back after ten years of activity
and one year of teaching as Dean Emeritus, I feel it
all was right--He planned it--I lived it.

Walter Houston Clark is the elder statesman of
contemporary psychologists of religion in America.
In a sense, he is today's William James, Harvard's
great psychologist in the early 1900's. Like James,
he has emphasized again and again the central place
of religious experience. He wrote one of the modern
classics in the field, The Psychology of Religion
(1958) and helped found the Society of the
Scientific Study of Religion. He served as its
first president. He taught at several institutions
and retired as Professor of the Psychology of
Religion at Andover Newton Theological School.

                    A Follower of William James
                              by
                     Walter Hauston Clark

At Harvard

In the early 1940's I was a graduate student in psychology at Harvard where William James had written his classic <u>The Varieties of Religious Experience</u> at the turn of the century.

I had long been curious as to what had been the long term effect of the religious experience many of my friends had had in the Oxford Group (or Moral Rearmment) when we were in college in the 1920's. Accordingly I proposed to Professor Gordon W. Allport, then Chairman of the Psychology Department, that I make such a study under his guidance. He was interested but declared that I would have difficulty in securing the approval of his department for any dissertation involving religion. When I insisted that I was much more interested in the study than in any degree, his response was that there ought to be some way in the university of William James by which a student interested in the psychology of religion could do a doctoral dissertation in the field.

Thus, he suggested a plan under which I would write the dissertation in the School of Education as a history of the Oxford Group in the colleges. Allport said, "You can bootleg into your thesis all the psychology that you want". Consequently, the work for my Ph.D. went through without a hitch and hardly a moment of dullness. Had I not secured it, I probably never would have been equipped to do work in the field of the psychology of religion, my main interest and enthusiasm.

The Oxford Group

Actually, it was my own religious experience I was studying in my dissertation. I, too, was deeply moved by the Frank Buchman evangelistic movement which became known as the Oxford Groul. As a student at Williams College I had attended several of their meetings on campus. Here I came in contact with those whose lives had been changed and redirected

through a vital religious movement. My own religious
life was deepened through the most vital religious
experience I had known up to that time, and even though
I had certain reservations concerning the Buchman emphasis, the experience was a large factor in my decision to desert science, my goal up to that time, and go
into the teaching of English at the secondary level.

In preparation for the latter, I entered Harvard
Graduate School in the fall of 1925.

The Lenox School

The years between the study at Harvard in the
1920's and the writing of the dissertation in the 1940's
were spent teaching English at the Lenox School for
Boys in western Massachusetts. The School was religiously oriented. Its philosophy was securely grounded
in Christian idealism and simple living. I was happy
there.

My love of literature was not strange. It had been
spawned by my mother, a kindergarten teacher. She was
imaginative and intuitive. Steeped in the Bible she
introduced me to religion by reading to me her favorite
psalms and narratives from both the Old Testament and
the New; Psalm 103 and John's Gospel, for example.
But she also was fond of reading me fairy tales, myths
and other stories of the marvels of fantasy. In particular I remember stories from Hawthorne's Tanglewood
Tales, Perseus and the Gorgon's Head, Jason and the
Golden Fleece, but particularly the story of Bellero-
phon and the winged horse Pegasus. Somehow, my mother
conveyed to me not only a sense of the wonder of existence but the idea that truer realities go far beyond
the surface appearance of things. This, as I now see it,
constitutes the central concept on which my life and
work has been predicated.

In my teaching both of the Bible and of literature
at Lenox, it was the notes of mysticism and of ecstasy
that struck the deepest chords within me. At that time
I could not have given a clear definition of mysticism,
while the word ecstasy in connection with my religion
would have frightened me to death. Yet here it was
clearly before my eyes in the drama of the Book of Job
the pages of Shakespeare, the prose poetry of Thomas
Carlyle, the symbolism of Tennyson, the haunting

passages of William Blake. Such reading strangely
moved me, yet far from being able to spell out the
reason, the whole was like a foreign tongue of whose
phrases I could only here and there discern the meaning.

During my days at Lenox there occurred another important happening that developed and broadened me. My
family was generally anti-Catholic. My father, though
he was much too gentle to dislike individual Catholics
whom he knew, had a fixed idea of the menace of the
Catholic Church. And his stand had its effect on me.
The agony involved in proposing to the warm and respon-
sive Catholic girl with whom I had fallen in love,
Ruth-Marie O'Brien of Milwaukee, did much to dent my
bias. My marriage to her was the start of many friendships with Catholic laymen and priests alike, and the
ghosts of my settled projudice seemed to have been
pretty well laid for good during the reign of Pope John
XXIII.

After Harvard

My dissertation helped me focus on my first love,
i.e. the psychology of religious experience. Although I
taught a variety of psychology courses, I was most motivated by the opportunity to teach the psychology of
religion. Middlebury College enticed me away from
Bowdoin with just such a promised opportunity.

After four years at Middlebury I went to Hartford
Seminary Foundation, where I was Professor of Psychology
and Dean at the Hartford School of Religious Education.
At that time the School had a semi-independent status
and an excellent reputation in its field. My life was
never busier. Besides my administration duties, I
taught a full load in the field of psychology with
emphasis on its religious aspects. I also provided
psychological counseling for students on the campus
who cared to see me relative to emotional problems.
And it was at Hartford that I wrote, over a period of
about four years, The Psychology of Religion. The book
had been suggested by a salesman who inspired me. It
was a distillation of my thinking and focused my
interests even more in the study of religious experience.

87

Drugs as Triggers of Religious Experience

In 1962 I resigned as Dean of the Hartford School
of Religious Education to accept a position as Professor
of Psychology of Religion at Andover Newton Theological
School in Newton Centre, Massachusetts. During a sabbatical at Andover Newton I had come in contact with the
work with psychedelic substances being done by Dr.
Timothy Leary at Harvard University.

It was his claim that the drugs, chiefly psilocybin
and LSD, triggered profound religious experience. I
started as a skeptic, having taken a dim view of this
possibility in The Psychology of Religion. But the
issue was one in my own field, and I felt that at the
very least it behooved me to be open-minded and learn
what I could from direct observation. Accordingly I
joined a seminar organized by Dr. Leary for scholars
and graduate students in the religious field. When he
made the statement that convicts at a maximum security
prison were talking like medieval mystics following
ingestion of psychedelic drugs, I sought confirmation
from some of my academic friends in the Department of
Social Relations at Harvard. The word I got from them
was that Leary did not know what he was talking about,
that his research with the convicts was a scandal, and
that everyone connected with it, including the convicts
were completely disillusioned.

This confused me. It was obvious that, if I were
to find what the truth was, I would have to find out
for myself. Accordingly, I accepted Dr. Leary's invitation to meet and talk with those of his subjects
who still remained in prison. I had not been behind
the prison walls fifteen minutes before I discovered
that, if anyone was disillusioned, it was certainly not
the convicts. Their accounts of their drug experiences
included many religious elements, some of a profound
nature.

One of the convicts, Donald M. Painten, a life-
long criminal serving a twenty year term for armed
robbery, had had a vision in which he had helped Christ
carry the cross toward Golgotha. The look of compassion that Jesus had given him in this vision shook him
to his foundations. He looked out of the prison window.
"All my life came before my eyes," he told me, "and I
said 'What a waste!'" Painten, along with another

convicted armed robber, James Kerrigan, also a subject
in the experient, started the Self-Development Group
for the rehabilitation of themselves and other convicts.
It already has saved the Commonwealth of Massachusetts
hundreds of thousands of dollars in reduced recidivism.
Painten has now been out of jail for over ten years
which, for him, is unprecedented. I know of no more
cogent example of the power of Christ in a man's life
than his.

However, though I recognize the great promise of
Leary's work with convicts as a pilot study, I do acknowledge one weakness of it, if one wishes thoroughly
to convince social scientists. It did not contain a
control group. People said, "Timothy Leary alone could
convert a stone. How do we know but that the trust he
developed and the attention he gave to the convicts was
the important factor, and not the drugs?" Certainly,
had he organized a similar group to whom he had given
equal time which, without the drugs, had done less well
on recidivism, it would have been harder for his Harvard
critics to dismiss his work as easily as they did.
However, Painten and other subjects told me very positively that though their trust in Leary was important,
without the drugs their reformation would have been
impossible.

This kind of evidence that the drugs could trigger
effective religious experience in at least some persons
engaged my interest. Personally, I was much impressed
and secured permission from the Massachusetts Commis-
sion on Correction to follow up Leary's study but with
a proper control group. However, public fear and
hysteria about the drugs, at least partly understandable, had made this, so far, impossible. It is a pity
that such a promising method of rehabilitating convicts, confirmed by experiments abroad, should so far
not have received a rigorous test in the United States.

Proof to Myself

About this same time, I received further confirmation of my growing belief that the drugs might have
religious properties. I was persuaded by Dr. Leary to
try the drugs. Accordingly, with other scholars and
colleagues, I sampled both LSD and psilocybin several
times. The experiences were not predominately mystical
as I had hoped. They partook mostly of the nature of
the "conviction of sin" in which a sense of my faults

impressed themselves upon me in a poignant, often
visionary form. Certain animosities dropped away
and have never come back. Biblical passages took on
an amazing freshness and vitality. I found myself
feeling very close to those with whom I shared the
experience. I, at least, learned what the mystics·were
talking about when they termed their experience ineff-
able. More than with my Buchmanite experiences, I can
say that from my firsthand encounter with the drugs,
the study of religion during a lifetime tòok on an
amazing freshness. This culminated with an experience
in Mexico with the psilocybe mushrooms in which I
"faced death" with a consequent experience of "rebirth."
Since then my zest for living has undergone a definite
intensification.

The Good Friday Experiment

     Capping my conversion to the initially unwelcome
idea of the religious agency of the drugs was the Good
Friday Experiment, probably the most carefully designed
and scientifically administered experiment in the
whole history of the psychology of religion. This com-
prised the doctoral study at Harvard of one of the
graduate students attracted to Leary's seminar. Dr.
Walter N. Pahnke already had an M.D. from Harvard Medical School and a B.D. from the Divinity School. Thus,
he was academically well equipped.

     Twenty volunteers from Andover Newton's Junior
class in 1962 were given identical preparation. Ten were
given psilocybin and ten a placebo, then, with the permission of Dean Howard Thurman, all attended a private
service on Good Friday at Boston University's Marsh
Chapel. The design was double blind. This means that
neither the subjects nor the experimenter and his
assistants knew who had received the drug and who had
received the placebo. Criteria of mystical experience
were set up before the experiment and applied by im-
partial judges.

     The results was that all but one of the experi-
mental group were judged to have reported characteristics of the mystical consciousness, even of them to a
high degree; while only one of the control group did
so, and he to only a mild degree. Even after six months
the follow-up indicated that the two groups were still
clearly differentiated, notably in their estimates of
beneficial effects on their lives subsequent to the

90

experiment. Statistically the conclusion that the
drugs touched off mystical experience was valid to an
exceedingly high degree. That I know of no experiment
in the difficult field of religious experience more
clear in its conclusions testifies to the high value of
the drugs as a means of achieving and studying the religious consciousness.

Further Research

Shortly after this came the formation of the
Neurobiological and Psychedelic Study Group started by
Professor Nuston Smith, Dr. Clemens Benda, and myself.
This was an informal gathering of scholars interested
in the drugs which met for several years at the
Massachusetts Institute of Technology. Through this, I
became connected with a research team from the Worcester
Foundation for Experimental Biology which, over two
summers, set up an experiment to give a few normal
volunteers LSD every day for up to sixteen days. The
purpose was to measure cyclical effects of the drug in
various physiological and psychological areas. My
function was to supervise the "trips" and to study religious aspects of the experiences.

I had devised a questionnaire for the study in
which I asked the subjects to compare their experiences
under the drug with their normal religious experiences.
Their ratings were graded in six degrees from zero to
five in which zero meant "no different from normal",
while five meant "beyond anything ever experienced or
imagined".

About one year later I followed up each subject in
an interview in which I asked him to fill out the
questionnaire from the perspective that time gave. Not
completely to my surprise, the category most often used
was "beyond anything ever experienced or imagined".
Five of the eight rated the significance of the total
experiment to them in this category while three gave it
a rating of three, "marked and intense". This gave
empirical support to what mystics universally testify.
Mystical experience is different in quality from ordinary consciousness and cannot adequately be described to
one who has not experienced it.

All eight reported clear indications of profound
religious experience in one form or another. Of the
three whose religious experience was rated as the most
intense, one was a theological student and two were
professed atheists! At first the latter were very

91

resistant to answering positively the question that used the concept of God, though in other ways they reported intense religious experience, perhaps without completely realizing it. But a year later they were willing to report the experience of God as extremely intense. While I would hardly describe their experience as completely orthodox, this strengthened my insight into the fact that many atheists are believers in reverse. If they knew or cared nothing about God they would hardly take the trouble to deny Him. Perhaps unconsciously they are rejecting lukewarm faith and so, unwittingly, doing God's work better than many a confessed believer. Much of my current thinking on this issue is included in my 1969 book Chemical Ecstasy.

A Time of Testing

My conviction of the revolutionary nature of the proper use of the psychedelic drugs in the field of psychotherapy, religion, and culture in general grew slowly but firmly. At the same time my respect for Dr. Leary also grew. Though my way of expressing interest in the drugs was more restrained and conventional than his, I saw him as so far ahead of his times that he was mistaken for a menace and harassed by the very society he sought to serve. As the result of his use of the psychedelic drugs, his deeply religious nature emerged. While no more faultless than any other human being, I see his essential integrity as absolute.

Consequently, when he began to have difficulties with the Harvard authorities over his research, I was one of those who counseled him to create his own research organization to save both him and Harvard embarrassment. I was asked to become one of the incorporators of the International Federation for Internal Freedom. On this account my name became publicized. After Dr. Leary's dismissal from Harvard, I was summoned before the president of the board of trustees of the institution I was then serving.[1]

The interview was a trying one. I was made to feel like a hostile witness under cross examination. I was

1. For an account of the affair at Harvard and a fuller appraisal of the character and personality of Dr. Leary see my Chemical Ecstasy, New York: Sheed, Andrew & Mc Meel, 1969, Chapter 4.

92

told I must resign immediately from the International Federation for Internal Freedom, promise never to mention the subject of drugs in any of my classes, and stop all experimentation with it or face summary dismissal by the trustees. I refused to bow to this grow violation of the principles of academic freedom. That the threat was never carried out was due to immediate support by my colleagues on the faculty and the tactful intervention of the president, Dr. Herbert Gezork, who was more aware of the principles of academic freedom than were the trustees. I will always continue to be grateful to these friends whose active confidence in me went far beyond routine support of my right to academic freedom in my field.

I have related this incident as an illustration to others of the claims on integrity that often confront the Christian teacher, as it often does other teachers as well.

Following my retirement I served briefly as Consultant at the Maryland Psychiatric Research Center, working there in creating research design and as a therapist in their program using LSD-types with alcoholics. Later I have become involved in observing and participating in the work of the gifted Mexican psychiatrist, Salvador Roquet. Dr. Roquet has combined the wisdom of Mexican Indian Shamans with western psychiatric techniques in developing a treatment modality which makes partial use of LSD-type drugs and plants. This combines religious values with depth therapy. It is the most effective therapy with which I am acquainted. My insight into Roquest's therapy has been further illuminated through attendance at an Indian peyote ceremony at which finally I achieved first hand insight into mystical ecstasy and its effects.

A Christian Psychologist

I am not retired but still active as a lecturer and researcher. There remains for me only to make a few general reflections on what I consider my function and message as a Christian psychologist.

I have heard it said by one noted scholar, that he had only developed one original idea, and then he had repeated that idea for the rest of his life. I cannot even claim the development of one original idea, however I can note a seed that has developed, strengthtned and then flowered in my teaching, so that I am sure my students have wearied in hearing it. From my earliest

childhood when my mother conveyed to me her conviction
of the reality of the unseen I have grown in my early
belief in the centrality of religion. For the individual I see his/her essential problem as an existential
one. It includes the facing of death, and thus life,
and the knowing who one is in the light of setting suns,
the blue oceans, the eternal rocks and the whole glorious
cosmos that frames our little day upon the earth.

For the bringing to birth in man of this knowing,
I see a complex process involving a strange relationship between the outer world and that inner world of
which Jesus said, "The kingdom of God is within you".
Part of this process involves our minds and the scientific rationality of which the western world is so
proud.

But something else is necessary. This something
else has been neglected in our search for power, outward security, and the rewards of our achieving society.
I speak of our nonrational functions. This is the
matrix out of which evolves poetry, art, music, and
finally the most captivating, illuminationg, and trans-
forming experience of which persons are capable: the
encounter with God. Though called by many names in
many faiths, it is God who summoned us out of the hard-
ness of the rock to a trembling and uncertain existence.
God is that Nothing, as Jonathan Edwards might put it,
"of which the sleeping rocks do dream".

This has led me to accept mamy things as possibilities, which even so short a time as twenty years ago I
might well have scorned. I am thinking here of such
things as faith healing, paranormal phenomena, and even
perhaps more esoteric things, so that I have adopted
as one of my maxims Hamlet's words, "There are more
things in heaven and earth than are dreamt of in your
philosophy".

Then in what sense do I consider myself a Christ-
tian? I have always tried to make myself available to
students whenever they have had need of me, and some of
the most satisfying moments in my career have been
those spent in counseling students or others in emotional distress. By believing in them and supporting them
I have been able to help them to help themselves. I
would like to think, as one not unprejudiced counselee
put it, that my faith in God persuaded me to stay out
of the way so that God might to the healing. Certainly the Christian psychologist should avoid the

besetting temptation of all counselors, that of playing God.

Mostly, however, I have performed the function of intellectual. In this I have tried to provide an intellectual framework of a psychological nature to help students conceptualize the power of the religious life. And partly because the intellectual approach to religion can become dessicated and dull, I have always tried to emphasize the place of religious experience. I believe in the importance of the mystical and the ecstatic for effective Christian living. Jesus was an ecstatic, as was Paul and other founders of our faith.

But I have never allowed myself to rest in the comfortable assurance that in conceptualizing my faith and merely studying it, my work as a Christian has been done. Christianity has to be lived, and that never can be done in cold blood. My task as an intellectual Christian I have always considered a necessity, though a humble one.

> All that I aspired to be,
> And was not, comforts me;

wrote Robert Browning. In a similar sense I suppose that my only claim to being a Christian lies in my knowing that I am not a very good one. If I had any pretense, my acquaintance with Don Painten, the armed robber whose escape from performing an act of murder lay mostly in his never finding himself in a situation where murder became a necessity, would bring me up short. With him, his visionary encounter with Christ is still a dynamic factor, keeping him from the only trade he has ever mastered--armed robbery. Still, after many years, its memory so deeply stirs him that he cannot tell about it without being moved. And yet he has hardly ever darkened the doors of a church!

Another example was one of my students, a woman, brought up in a typical middle class suburban family whose church was one of its lowest priorities. Yet some invisible force through the years seemed to draw her toward God. Finally, in middle age she was overtaken by a religious experience of mystical intensity. Currently she serves a church. Like the Hound of Heaven, it is as if Christ had been pursuing her over the years. Now, living on a pittance, the chief thing that distresses her is that the church as an institution is so needless of Him. People like her teach me the shallowness of my own Christian comitment.

I once asked the late Paul Tillich how he explained the apparent paradox that many non-Christians were models of Christlike compassion, while many Christians were predatory, self-seeking, and cruel. His answer was that the non-Christians I described were still "new men in Christ" by which he meant new men by the standard of Christ.

This statement of Tillich pretty well presents my own case. Many of the best "Christians" I know are friends of other faiths whose Christlike spirits put me to shame.

However, I happen to have been brought up as a Christian, and my allegiance is to Christ. He is the human being who for me most concretely speaks of God. He is the touchstone who helps to correct me when I go wrong. His are the principles that enable me to describe the essence of those friends whose love is so much stronger than my own. What little influence for good my career as a Christian psychologist has had has been defined and focussed by my allegiance to Him.

A TARDY PILGRIM

by

Mary Jo Meadow

Dr. Mary Jo Meadow is Associate Professor of Psychology at Mankato State University, Minnesota where she is director of the graduate program in clinical psychology. She has had long standing interest in research in the psychology of religion and is presently co-authoring a volume in this field. She has been active in The Society for the Scientific Study of Religion, The American Academy of Religion, and Psychologists Interested in Religious Issues, one of the newest Divisions of the American Psychological Association.

Dr. Meadow grew up in the Roman Catholic Church but found herself increasingly unable to reconcile some practices of worship and morality with her own evolving viewpoints. She speaks of herself as a "tardy" pilgrim in the sense that she never left the Christian faith in her heart and has found it incorporated into her spiritual journey through her research, writing, and personal worship. She writes of this saga in a manner that will be familiar to many behavior scientists who have wrestled with their faiths.

A Tardy Pilgrim

I studied to be both an academic and a clinical
psychologist and now work in both these arenas. I
hold an appointment in a state university where I
teach a wide variety of psychology courses: introductory, personality, psychopathology, clinical
assessment, mental health, aging, psychology of women -
and religion. I am involved in training future
clinical psychologists and also have a small private
practice doing clinical assessment, psychotherapy,
and marriage counseling.

Although my major academic training was in
personality and clinical psychology, psychology of
religion is my sub-specialty and most of my research
work is in this area. My major project to date is
developing a religious attitudes inventory which I
use in my ongiong research. I am especially interested in understanding patterns of religious feelings
and beliefs and in the relationship between these and
mental health. I am also writing a textbook of
psychology and religion with another Christian psychologist who has influenced me profoundly.

My favorite teaching assignment is psychology
of religion. Since people who are attracted to such
a class at a state university usually have some
personal problems or concerns in this area, the
classes come to be experiences of personal growth -
as well as academic learning - for many of my students.
The task I have been given in this article parallels
an assignment that I have been giving my religion
students for years: writing an autobiographical
account of one's own spiritual pilgrimage.

I am one of those people who exemplify the
statement of psychologist Gordon Allport that
people raised in families where there is deep religiousness usually have strong religious interests as
adults. Although I have rejected many of the religious positions of my parents, religion remains an
intense concern in my life. My parents were what would

now be considered pre-Vatican II Catholics. Their faith was strongly dogmatic, legalistic, and miracle-seeking. Early in life I ran into collisions with them over religious perspectives. I recall as early as eleven years of age having arguments over points of belief that they interpreted literally and which appeared to me absurd. I also questioned cherished practices of theirs which I considered superstitious.

Prior to these disagreements with my parents, I grew up deeply involved in religion. Some of my earliest reading, in which I greatly delighted, was biographies and writings of Christian saints. I was thrilled by their disciplines and tried in small ways to imitate some of the less esoteric ones. My parents asked frequently if I was staying "in the state of grace" and I went through periods of intense scrupulosity, being certain I made my confessor understand the exact nature and extent of my sinfulness. The importance of attending Mass and receiving communion for nine consecutive first Fridays of the month - a guarantee of salvation as it supposedly ensured a priest's presence when you died - was so emphasized that I completed this practice several times "just to be sure." My parents spent much time debating such issues as whether it was permissible to eat canned beans with pork on Friday if you did not eat the pork piece. They had an all-consuming interest in the latest appearances of the Virgin Mary to warn humans of their sinfulness. People who owned such items as tears shed by statues, roses that never died (from a religious shrine), relics of saints, and various healing waters and oils were welcome guests in our home.

By my mid-teens I was close to complete abandonment of the religious endeavor. One crucial experience was a pilgrimage my family took to a place where the Virgin Mary was allegedly appearing. I was literally nauseated by the sight of people hawking cheap plastic rosaries for high prices and the general carnival atmosphere of the whole scene. I identified religiousness with my parent's type of religion and did not want anything to do with it. This was in part rationalization; I also strongly disliked the restraints that religion put on my conduct and wanted to be free to do a number of forbidden

things. In order to avoid upsetting confrontations
with my parents, I continued the outward practice
of their religion until I left home at eighteen.

After several years of college, my early spiritual hungers flared up again and I began to explore
religion. I encountered clergymen whose orthodox
scholasticism and casuistry did not "insult my intelligence" as I considered my family's religion to do.
I found myself embracing a very different Catholic
perspective - on a very intellectual and uncommitted
plane. This religion of social and intellectual
respectability continued into my early years of
marriage.

An increasing void in my life soon led me into
a depression of several years' duration. As I became more deeply depressed I became less and less
capable of religious belief as I had previously
understood it, while desperately longing for it. I
remember angrily challenging heaven, "If you're up
there, at least make it possible for me to believe
it since I need to so much." I interpreted all my
problems as due to my inability to believe that
spiritual reality really existed. All my previous
rational arguments and complicated reasoning failed
to convince me. Finally I became desperate enough
that one evening I lay down on my bed and resolved
to stare at the ceiling until I went out of my mind.
When I woke the next morning I was frightened enough
that I knew I had to do something. I decided to
heal myself by acting "as if" and threw myself into
many volunteer and religious efforts. I painfully
went through the motions while deeply aware of the
heavy and dead core within myself. Yet I spoke of
it to no one.

At a retreat which was proving a deadly and
boring experience, the priest leader let his mind
wander during the rosary and badly lost his place.
When he took the pulpit he acknowledged this to the
assembly. That this small act of humility impressed
me as much as it did says much about how proudly
I was unable to admit any insufficiency or weakness
to anyone elso. Convinced that this priest, Father
Pat, would be able to help me, I asked him for an

appointment. When we met I talked about the weather, religious education, liturgy changes - I talked about everything except what I had come to talk about. I went home bitterly angry at God, him, and myself. In desperation, I phoned him and told him that I had talked about everything except what I needed to, and requested another appointment.

This time I succeeded and it all came out: my spiritual past, the empty dryness, the inability to make myself feel that metaphysical reality conformed to my desires - even some of the anger over my inability to believe while trying so hard to. After listening patiently, he started explaining that religious faith did not work the way I expected, that it could never be a matter of logically reasoning to certain conclusions. He said that one has to be willing to gamble in faith, that persons of faith must stake their entire life upon a vision without any absolute certainty that it is true. He told me by problem was not one of faith, but rather of love. I had never before been exposed to such an understanding of religion and it thoroughly frightened me. I could not get out of there fast enough. I remember driving my car that evening - well over the speed limit - down one of the city's main streets until it dead-ended in the country.

I sat in my car in the dark and argued with God, crying and screaming. It wasn't fair that one could not even have the consolation of knowing that something was true if they were supposed to live by it! I was willing to try so hard - all I wanted was to know that it was not in vain. Dammit, I just wanted some little sign that something important existed outside of the here and now! Time passed; I grew less angry, but more weary and frightened. How could I stand to live if it weren't true? That was an unbearable thought; it simply had to be true. More time passed; it was getting very late. Finally, "Okay, God, you win. I'll try. I'll give. I want you enough to gamble. Don't give me anything; just let me give. All I'll ask for is that you sustain me. Just let me given to you."

So I went back to my life. I tended my family; I did my volunteer work. I still did not "believe." But the dead place inside me had been replaced by a small kernel of serenity. And somehow I was suddenly

101

patient and kind. Somehow I had energy to do my
work without my previous utter exhaustion; my depression was gone. I was lifted out of my deeply
engrossed egocentricity and forgot about myself as
I cared for others. I opened myself completely -
all my guilts, my sins, my lackingness - to Father
Pat. In all other people, I tried to see God.

And then, within a few weeks, I did "see" God.
How does one write about ecstatic religious experience -
what can one say if she tries to describe the indescribable? I was in church late one afternoon re-
peating, as I often did, my prayer of self-offering
with the request only for sustainment. And then
I suddenly "disappeared" - so did the church, time, and
everything else except God. I do not know how long
it lasted, but in prayer - buried in a darkness in
which I could not see, a vacuum in which I could not
hear, in a spaceless-timeless void - I "saw" God, I
"heard" God, and I was "in" God. When I again
became aware of my surroundings it was dark outside and
my limbs were stiff and strained. But I was "wrapped"
in God and carried a sphere of light, warmth, and
indescribable peace around me. And I "believed" -
I believed with a belief so removed from a child's
naive acceptance of Santa Claus that the same word
should not be used to describe both.

Thus began several years of the most intense
experiences of my entire life. Throughout every
day, God was "with" me as a tangible presence. And
daily, through Christ, I quenched my thirst at that
fountain in the dark and silent void - some days
one hour, some days two. And the people began to
come to me. First the teenagers I taught in church
school, with their problems and aspirations. And
then the adults - the ones the priests could not
talk to and sent to me: the depressed, the angry, the
suicidal, the confused, the "sinners." Each went
away from me with something that seemed more to pass
through me than come from me and each came back for
more; gradually they began to get pulled together.

After several years I decided I should learn how
to do what I was doing, so I went back to school with
two purposes in mind: to acquire skills as a psychotherapist and to study religion from a psychological

102

perspective. There began to be more time for study and less time for patience with other people. Less interest in prayer and more concern for my grade point average. And some problems in Catholicism became increasingly apparent to me. A series of crises of conscience began: Catholic education for my children in a school whose atmosphere repelled me, birth control, compulsory ritual with a feeling of people being "processed through", bishops living in palaces and encouraging the war in Southeast Asia - the list seemed endless. So, in a series of con- science-wrenching steps, I left Catholicism.

I continued some remnant of my practice of interior prayer, but found myself in disquieting places with it at times. Shortly after I left the church, my spiritual guide left town and I knew of no one else with whom I could discuss these things. With my increasing psychological sophistication, I was also becoming wary. Experiences such as mine were reported by people with many different trigger- ing circumstances. Are these really a breakthrough to some reality beyond? Are they the projecting creation of an "Other" to whom one can relate? Are they a return to some state of undifferentiated consciousness? Are they a mere trick of the mind? My attitude of unself-seeking self-abandonment had vanished; I was again asking questions and wanting answers.

I became spiritually adrift. School filled time, then teaching, clinical internship, and research. I continued to become less and less giving, more and more self-engrossed. What I was doing and what I wanted to do was of paramount importance. Prayer was almost completely abandoned, although with a nostal- gic tug I often thought about it. Yet when I tried, the magic of being bathed in God did not occur. The God-concept was increasingly anchored to an amorphous and vague content of which I felt less and less sure. And gradually I sickened of myself. I did not like the impatience and jealousy and self- centeredness I saw when I looked at myself. I thirs- ted for the righteousness and cleanness of heart I had seemed to have for those few fleeting years.

103

So, with a quiet despair, I again began imploring
God (or my own finer inner self, or the Tao, or the
Ground of Being, or the impersonal underlying law -
I knew not what to call it or how to consider it). In
my innermost being a constant petition was chanted: for
goodness, for completeness, for sincerity and truth,
for lovingness. And I met Panditji (a yoga teacher or
guru) who impressed me much as Father Pat had some
years before. I turned to him imploringly with my
whole tale of sickness of myself and my desire to
transcend this narrowness. And he welcomed me and
warmed me.

Again I had one fleeting experience of that
timeless-spaceless void from which I emerged with the
deep peace of perfect serenity - to last for a while.
But my selfishness did not fall away this time as
it had the last and I was to taste of no more immediate
spiritual sweetness. I was full of doubt about what
I was trying to accomplish. Faith, hope, and love
did not blossom spontaneously; caution, stubbornness,
and entrenched little pettinesses did not yield. One
night I dreamed I was dressed in pilgrim clothing
walking barefoot over rocky, hot, sun-baked hills in
the heat of noon; beside me walked a silent monk, a
half-step behind me, a speechless goad pushing me on.
So I took a deep breath and decided that it had to
be the rocky road this time. I had chosen to leave
Paradise and now the gates were closed.

And I had another dream - the most beautiful of
my entire life. I was riding in a whale (Jonah?)
with many other people. We were sitting in deck
chairs in the side of the whale, with his side open
to the sea in front of us. A Model-T Ford (cautious
and stubborn old remnants?) was being towed on a
raft behind. We were waiting - waiting interminably.
I was suffering dreadfully with waiting - longing,
parched, and yearning. Then a magnificent fish swam
up alongside the whale and gave me a look of infinite
compassion and understanding. It said, "Why did you
doubt me, oh you of little faith?" and then rolled
over. Its underbelly was spread with an immense
feast of the finest banquet imaginable.

I held onto the implied promise of this dream and
continued my interior pleas. "Let the seed die that

104

it may sprout new life." Or, "Let me be resigned
to having the seed die, regardless of what happens to
it, even if that is nothing." I adopted yogic discipline, but applied it sporadically. I joined a
small Christian fellowship circle in which the members
shared with each other their successes and failures
in living the gospel. I rediscovered a quotation
from deChardin which had been on my dresser mirror
for over a dozen years:

> ...what is sanctity in a creature if not to
> cleave to God with the maximum of his strength?
> and what does that maximum cleaving to God
> mean if not the fulfillment...of the exact
> function, be it lowly or eminent, to which
> that creature is destined both by nature
> and by supernature? (from The Divine
> Milieu, p. 36)

I found myself gradually realizing again that,
for me, divinity is most clearly manifest in Christ.
Now it did not matter to me that my intense emotional
conditioning to Christian symbols was probably responsible for this. I also realized that for me
religion had to be clearly grounded in personal
religious experience: my yogic affiliation offered
the same basic practices and principles that I had
encountered in the Christian mystical tradition.
This communality across traditions did not dilute, but
rather enhanced, the importance of this aspect of
religiousness. I recognized that I had come to value
and appreciate the religious experience of people
from widely varying perspectives - at the cost of
losing my capacity for the security of certainty.
I realized that I could never again wholeheartedly
embrace a legalistic morality and was condemned to
the "insecurity" of full responsibility for my own
moral decisions.

When I asked Panditji for guidelines for moral
decision-making, he gave me four. First, consult
the scriptures. (When I commented that you can
always read them to say what you want to hear, he
smiled and said, "Of course.") Second, consult a
spokesperson for tradition. (When I commented that
different ones say different things, he smiled and
said, "Of course.") Third, ask yourself it it really
feels right to you. Finally, if it does feel right,

ask yourself if you are willing to pay, <u>without</u>
<u>resentment</u>, the cost of the decision. Some might
pejoratively call it antinomianism, but I have
found no advice for moral decision-making I consider
superior to Panditji's. When I duscussed with him
my inability to decide which fork of a certain moral
dilemma to take, he told me to sit in the crossroads
and learn patience until I felt right about one of
the paths. I sat on this particular dilemma (divorce)
for several years.

I had not yet made my peace with the Christian
church. That was some years in coming and began
largely because of the influence of other Christian
psychologists who saw value in the church. Because
of my closeness to Catholicism, I was more aware of
its weaknesses than those of other denominations,
yet was certain they all had crucially important
ones. I have grown more understanding of organizational
foibles and realize that I can now tolerate many things
that at one point I could not. I have not become a
member of any church, but am not opposed to so doing.
If ever it seems appropriate, I will join a church
and adopt its worship and disciplines.

Currently I regularly attend churches of many
denominations, including my formerly abandoned Catholic one. I find I can worship with all these groups
and could probably affiliate with many of them comfortably. Until I returned to church, I was not aware
of how much of a gap was left in my religiousness
without Christian worship. My main sustenance in
religion, however, still lies in the interior prayer
tradition. I still retain my yogic affiliation and
some of its disciplines.

I am a much different person from the young
woman who twenty years ago sought an understandable
and explainable God. I am also much different from
the ardent young mystic of several years later who
poured herself out in self-abandoned service. I
sometimes think of this latter as a loss, probably in
part for the self-seeking reason that I miss the
uncomplicated faith I had and still yearn for those
personal visits to "heaven" which I no longer have
with any predictability or regularity. Yet I
realize that I found it necessary to leave Eden and

and to taste the fruit of the tree of knowledge. If this means that belief must necessarily be heuristic, that moral decision-making is fraught with ambiguity, that loving behavior sometimes costs dearly, that self-denial is difficult, that ritual does not always hold its magic, that prayer may be painful and dry, that the religious vision is usually "through a glass darkly", and that the whole venture is filled with many failures, then it means simply that I am embedded in the full human condition.

I believe all the life circumstances in which I find myself are my spiritual task. This begins with the intelligence and special talents with which I was born. Developing these that they may be instruments of service, rather than personal assets to be clung to, is part of my calling. My work as a psychologist - to which I was strongly drawn by the circumstances of my life - is clearly part of vocation. The students in my classroom, the psychotherapy clients in my office, the research problems that present themselves - all are part of my stewardship. The effort I spend with each of these is part of my gift back from that entrusted to me.

Personal relationships are a very important part of the religious calling for me, the part most difficult of all to manage. It is in relationships that impatience, irritabiligy, stinginess, insensitivity, and self-seeking get most in the way of the calling to live with others in Christian love. Sometimes all we can do is to turn to one another in sincerity and penitence with mutual forgiveness, support, and encouragement.

Although I see my active and busy life as my current spiritual task, I seek another calling - with some of the tenor of my years of self-abandonment - for the future. After some years, I hope to retreat from my fully active life to one of more prayer and simple service. This clearly will involve use of my skills as a psychologist and the calling upon whatever wisdom I have managed to acquire. Although not originally spurred by it, this is supported by yogic spirituality which calls for some years of a "retreat to the forest" between the years of active full participation in life and those years

107

spent in fuller renunciation before death.

Some consider my religiousness a hodge-podge.
I am unwilling to discard anything I have found to
be of value, regardless of where I found it. This
means that my Christianity is permeated with Eastern
yogic influence. It means that my enthusiasm for
any denomination's r tuals and disciplines is tempered
by my awareness of value I have seen in other denominations. It means that I have not undertaken a commitment to a specific tradition of Christian practice,
but choose both to support and draw from many. In
some respects this makes my religiousness highly
individualistic, yet I seek an intense spiritual
fellowship with those who become my close friends,
both influencing them and allowing myself to be influenced by their wisdom and goodness.

Although I have proved to myself that I am not
capable of indifference to religious endeavor, I
clearly do not uncritically accept all manifestations
of religiousness. I believe that religion can represent both the heights and the depths of human endeavor.
It can be the most demanding, most uplifting, and
highest task in which one can involve self. It can
be used to meet the grossest neurotic needs and to
endorse the perversion of all that the core message
of religion stands for. It can be a conscientious
commitment which pervades and colors one's entire
life. It can be an unthinking habit. And so on.
For most of us, it probably reflects a number of
both positive and negative characteristics. For those
of us who take it seriously, one area of religious
endeavor is the purification of the religious intention itself, the purging of the self-seeking in it
which is contrary to the message of all religions.

My current religious perspective is illustrated
my recent conservations I have had with two clergymen.
One tried to convince me that I must feel certain
that I am going to heaven. He could not understand
that such an assurance was not the reason for my
religious involvement. The other saw immediately
what I was trying to say. He commented, "Ah, yes,
you are saying that the payoff is in the doing itself."
Apparently I have at least traveled some distance

108

from my starting point. God, my friends, and I
all know at least some of the distance I have yet
to go.

Reference

de Chardin, Pierre Teilhard, The Divine Milieu,
    New York: Harper & Row, 1960.

V.

THE SELF AND CHRISTIAN FAITH

Much modern psychology is dominated by a concern with the self. We hear much about the self-concept, about self-confidence, about self-esteem, and about self-centeredness. The achievement of selfhood is felt by many to be what it means to be a person. Self-actualization is the term often used by many psychologists to stand for this important emphasis on finding one's own unique identity.

A number of Christian psychologists have occupied themselves with these issues. Dr. Finch shares a life long search for a psychological theory which is true to the self and true to the person of Jesus Christ. His central concept for a Christian psychology is anxiety which he feels is a sign of the self's effort to find itself. Dr. Fitts has given much of his time to a researching of the self-concept. He has designed a scale to measure persons' feelings about many aspects of their selves. He is convinced of the lasting importance of faith in the shaping of persons' selves.

Through their attempts to study, think about, measure, and express Christian selfhood, these psychologists illustrate yet another avenue through which psychology and faith can be related.

John G. Finch is a psychologist in private
practice in Tacoma, Washington. He has long sought
to detail and delimit a Christian psychology. He
suggests that "Christ is at the heart of psychology".
In the early 1960's, Dr. Finch began to be interested in training Christian psychologists. This interest led him to Fuller Theological Seminary where he
became one of the major forces in the establishment
of the Graduate School of Psychology. He continues
to teach each year at Fuller in addition to his
private practice. An annual lecture series at the
Seminary is named in his honor.

In Quest of a Christian Psychology
by
John S. Finch

My first contact with psychology was a chance
remark made by an observant teacher, R.S.B. Anderson
when I was in high school in India. Later in college,
I found myself devouring the subject and reading far
beyond the requirements of the course. It would be
assuming too much to suspect that I adequately appreciated all I read. However, being already quite
thoroughly familiar with the Scriptures, insights began to burst through in regard to the parallels that
existed between all the varieties of psychology I was
reading and these writings. The struggle to integrate
my Christian faith and the psychological systems seemed elusive. One thing remained constant: psychology
and the Christian faith were not antithetical even
though both camps insisted they had nothing in common.
I could exchange insights from one field to the other,
but at what point could I facilitate some real dis-
logue? Psychology seemed to discount the Christian
faith along with all other religions, and the Christian faith was "appropriately" defensive and condemned
psychology. Neither appeared to want anything to do
with the other. One seemed satisfied to take a stand
on scientific grounds, while the other appealed to
revelation for its priority. In the face of my own
confusion, this bifurcation was unacceptable to me.
Imbued with a vital inner witness of the Spirit on the
one hand, and a psychological awareness of personal
repressions and failures on the other, I was torn be-
bween the validity of the one and the vitality of the
other. The search persisted.

In 1940 I completed my Masters' degree in Philosophy and Psychology. The problem became more press-
ing. At this point I turned to psychoanalysis. Professor H.P. Maiti in the Department of Psychology at
the University of Calcutta accepted me for a didactic
analysis. Here, I felt, I could approach the problem
well as comprehend, in part, the interactions of psychology with my faith.

Dr. Maiti was a Freudian raised in the Hindu tradition. I was a committed Christian. Religion did not officially enter the arena, but of course all kinds of innuendoes emerged. My graduation and subsequent transfer from calcutta ended my formal analysis, but not my ability and desire, to explore myself and my religious dynamics.

At this time I went into the full-time ministry. I felt compelled to be relevant as I brought the gospel to my people. Harry Emerson Fosdick's The Meaning of Persons and Henry C. Link's My Return to Religion were most useful adjuncts in facilitating the way. Leslie D. Weatherhead and the writings of E. Stanley Jones gnawed away at the problem but still did not provide me a handle.

By the time I came to the United States in 1946, I had one educational objective; to acquire a Ph.D. at Drew University under Professor Edwin Lewis and to write a dissertation on the subject The Psychology of Jesus. From a revelational standpoint, I felt certain that if Jesus' thoughts around psychology could be pulled together, a system could be explicated that would surpass all others.

My hopes were frustrated. Professor Lewis claimed little knowledge of psychology. He directed me to Professor Stanley R. Hopper in the Department of Christian Ethics. He was to become my mentor and one to whom I owe an enormous debt. His encyclopaedic grasp of relevant issues inspired and guided my interests, and his method of teaching was the catalyst that brought to focus years of research and learning. Under his guidance I sorted out the nature of man in Freud, Adler, Otto Rank, Jung, James Jackson Putnam and, parenthetically Binswanger. It was a most exhilarating search.[1] Two essentials emerged: (1) Freud's scientism contaminated his own research and created a split in his work; while (2) even in Freud, a dimension in man was revealed which, strangely enough, both Freud and the dissenters had in common. For want of a better term, I have chosen to call it the dimension of "spirit".

But what is spirit, came the question? The more I explored the phenomena the more evident it became that spirit is that quality that characterizes man as self-transcendent, free and responsible. It is unique to persons.

114

Where did this lead in terms of the Christian faith? Did the "spirit-dimension" in psychology have any bearing on the body-soul-spirit in Christian Theology? Once again the trek began. Several theologians were explored for an understanding of the nature of man and the dimension of spirit; i.e., Nicholas Berdyaev, Emil Brunner, Reinhold Neibuhr, Soren Kierkegaard, etc. All of them seemed to concur in speaking of the nature of spirit as a person's freedom and selfhood. Here, at last, I felt I had discovered the missing link between psychology and theology.

But the question that still remained was one of methodology. Psychology was presenting itself as a science on a par with the other sciences and as capable of fully utilizing the scientific method. Theology, at best, in my view, is not subject to such methods. Even Kierkegaard had separated these two disciplines for the same reason. Indeed, the psychology with which he was familiar had a strong materialistic bent and was doing its utmost to imitate the medical and engineering models.[2] I had to come to a crucial decision. Could I accept the scientific method as adequate for an understanding of the nature of man? My answer, in conformity with numerous scientists, caused me to reject the scientific method as the answer. This I have spelled out rather fully elsewhere.[3]

Having rejected the hard-science method, I turned to an existential approach to knowledge. What I mean by this is that knowledge far transcends the gathering of factual data, of analysis and replication; that the notion of eliminating variables to control the data is too much like the Procrustean bed. When science is used to comprehend the nature of man, it poses a crippling strain on the method and distorts the subject--persons. Besides as more and more scientists are observing, (e.g. Michael Polany) so-called scientific objectivity has long been exploded as a myth.

It seems to me that the answer to a person's problems are not in trips to the moon, gadgets, abundance, affluence, etc. These are what Pascal might call "divertissement". Man can neither be understood nor healed by any form of materiality or materialism. "Man does not live by bread alone" is a wise saying and when science attempts to make man conform to a method, it reduces his stature as man.

115

I prefer the existential direction as portrayed by Kierkegaard. His main argument was a rejection of the rational as the way of knowing in favor of knowledge via experience. This seemed, then and indeed now to have the complete endorsement of Jesus who said: "If any man will do His will, he shall know the doctrine" Jn.7:17.

Having in my own thinking removed psychology from the limitations of the scientific method, I now set about to constitute what I call a Christian Psychology with particular relevance to therapy or healing. If man is man, therapy must be seen not as the removal of symptoms, but rather a change from an inadequate philosophy of life to a more complete and all-embracing philosophy of life. Therapy must be relevant to man as spirit, and made, as the theologians point out, "in the image of God." Therapy assumes the function of understanding persons in their refusal to be fully human. It must probe the ways in which persons in all their deviousness ingeniously create defenses against being persons. Here is where, for instance, Freud did religion a tremendous service in pointing to the various defenses man uses in refusing to be man while still expecting to reap the benefits of his full humanity--his identity as a spiritual being. Freudian theory fell down, however, when Freud insisted on using the medical model and construing man in terms of biology and materialistic determinism. Behaviorism has done us an ingenious service in specifying how "to train up a child in the way that he should go." But it has done us an enormous disservice in its philosophy that man is nothing but a stimulus-response mechanism.

A telling illustration of this damage was brought to my notice by a patient of mine who has been a highly successful job of child training in the school system. He expressed himself as having lost all feeling and enthusiasm and "if they kicked me out tomorrow, I could not care less". He was young and honest enough to recognize that the things we do to others affects us, i.e. to dehumanize is to become dehumanized. Man needs more than corrective measures to modify inappropriate behaviour. He needs to discover the inner dynamics that have allied themselves with a false world view or philosophy of life and then to find, voluntarily, with his defenses peeled away, a new and distinctively human philosophy of life that respects his nature as Spirit, as made

116

in the image of God, before he can function to his
fullest capacity.

I see this philosophy best lived out in Jesus
Christ. Hence, I sponsor a Christian Psychology. This
Jesus saves men in this all0comprehending and comprehensive way. Quite clearly and uniquely, He has done
something that no one ever did or can do for us. He
calls us to follow Him. Our acknowledgment of His
work on the cross and acceptance of that work for us
is demonstrated by our total commitment to that example -- (model), if you please). Sin, then, is
man's effort to show he has a better way and a more
comprehensive answer. He becomes bogged down by his
egocentricity which I suggest is the essence of all
emotional problems. And, the more defensive circles
he draws and tightens around himself, the more sick he
becomes. Psychosis is the deadly and ultimate outcome of his egocentricity.

"Where can one go to be taught this kind of
psychology?" This was the question numerous students
thrust at me in 1961 when I gave three lectures on
Christian Psychology at Fuller Theological Seminary.
Let me briefly outline what took place.

The Seminary's director of public relations
came to my office in Tacoma and asked if I would lecture at Fuller on my notion of Christian Psychology.
I accepted, with fear and trembling.

Before the entire faculty and student body and
in the presence of Dr. Charles E. Fuller, founder of
the Seminary, I delivered three lectures on my ideas
of a Christian psychology. My answer to their question: "Where can one go to be taught this kind of
psychology" was: "there is no school that I know of.
We will have to found our own school".

Dr. Paul Fairweather, at that time Professor of
Pastoral Counseling in the Seminary, adopted me and
the idea. I interacted to his inquiries before his
class at every opportunity. Mrs. Annette Weyer-
haeuser sat in all of these audiences. Her intellectual comprehension of the idea would have been enough,
but she had also experienced the integration in her
own being. I later received the message through her:
"If you can establish a school of psychology pattern-
ed after these ideas, I will put up a million dollars."

117

The idea had never been put forth before in our knowledge, so we had to start from scratch. In outline, the program, as I had considered it, envisaged a Graduate School of Psychology. In order to give students proper perspective they would be required to have a B.D. level of theological competence and also to go through the full program of a graduate level psychology. The assumptions were: (1) that in the intrapsychic interaction of these two disciplines the student would be exposed to the personal struggle and conflict of integration; (2) that if ever the Christian faith was to become a vital force in psychological practice it could only be explicated by men accepted by the profession as one of them; (3) that we would have our own clinical facility in which teachers and students could serve the emotionally disturbed with an emerging Christian psychology so that theory and practice could be integrated as well; (4) that this kind of professional psychologist could stand his ground in private practice, in churches, and institutions, as a demonstration and demonstrator of the nature of man as spirit.

In December, 1961 at a Fuller Board of Trustees and Faculty meeting in Santa Barbara, California, I was asked to present the notion that had been spawned in my lectures that previous May. I sensed no little incredulity and quite some defensiveness as I spoke, and I would have dismissed my reactions as paranoia if no expressions were verbalized. But these were aired quite freely.

The voting was favorable but large questions still existed. What kind of curriculum, in greater detail, should be followed? Exactly where should the school be located in the already cramped campus at Fuller? Where could we possibly find a faculty that had B.D.'s and Ph.D.'s in psychology? Whom could we find of sufficient stature to be Dean? What about student prospects? All we could do was to move ahead, a step at a time by faith.

In 1964, under the direction of Dr. Donald F. Tweedle, we opened the Pasadena Community Counseling Center. I was privileged to deliver an opening lecture on <u>Christianity as Insight</u>. The program was launched.

Many questions concerned us, including choice of a Dean. But, if God had had anything to do with my own years of preparation and the monetary assistance, He

118

was also working on a Dean. Indeed, He had already
spoken to a scientific skeptic through this skeptic's
interest in what he chose to call a "monument to sup-
erstition"--Bel Air Presbyterian Church, being built
on the hilltop where he lived. Dr. Lee Edward Travis,
clinical psychologist and neuropsychologist, and his
wife went to see this "monument" out of curiosity.
Dr. Louis Evans, Jr. was preaching that morning. Travis
felt no need to marshall defenses to refute "nothing".
So, in his posture of non-scientific curiosity, God
outflanked him as he found tears rolling down his
cheeks. He was the vessel prepared for our project.
My own feelings of inadequacy, after giving birth to
this infant, could only see adoption as its ground of
survival. To all his other prestigious qualifications,
God had moved in with a vital religious experience.
But what I saw as one of the most dynamic factors in
him was his total lack of theological sophistication.
This would bring a freshness and uniqueness to the task
of integration as it went on inside of him.

How Dr. Travis became known to us is a coincidence
par excellence. A former seminary student who was in
therapy with Dr. Travis took him a publicity brochure
about our new school. Dr. Travis was impressed and
agreed to meet with us when we called him. Paul Fairweather and I continued our "missionary journey", In a
dark restaurant in Beverly Hills once again the story
was told. I felt an inner response. I knew we had
found the Dean. I conveyed this to him. Travis demurred
on the grounds of his total lack of formal education in
theology. I was increasingly convinced. After all,
this man was already wrestling with the problem of
integration. His own experience of Christian vitality
and psychological understanding and experience were
the becrock of my original idea. Then too, from an
existential point of view, every man not only must,
but does, constitute his own theology. Not, of course,
apart from and devoid of the mass of Christian data,
but in experimenting with and experiencing it. This
then also gave him an opportunity for interaction
with theology. After one more interview, Travis
accepted and another formidable obstacle had been overcome.

In 1965 the school officially opened for the fall
quarter. Students and faculty had the faith to engage
themselves in the idea of integrating theology and
psychology. These men really saw the vision with

119

sufficient clarity and conviction to commit themselves
with courage to an untried, unproved dream. Amid the
confusion of newness and growing pains, they remained
steadrast and things began to fall into place. Professionals in the area have become increasingly
friendly. Training facilities have enveloped the students. The students seemed to have an unusual quality
about them. Indeed, they did. It could be summed up in
the words "Christian commitment and a calling to serve
God and mankind". This may be variously interpreted,
but the phenomenological fact is--the students brought
a new and distinctive flavor to their task. What I
had envisaged and predicted about having something
unique to offer in this integration was already being
demonstrated. The climax came in 1969 when the Western
Schools Accreditation Committee accredited our project
with the right to confer the Ph.D. degree.

How, it may be asked, does integration work in
clinical practice? How does it work in my practice?
My starting point has been a deep confrontation with
The Concept of Dread and The Sickness Unto Death by
Soren Kierkegaard. Kierkegaard starts from the point
of anxiety. Anxiety results from the possibility of
freedom in the face of alternatives and the necessity
for choice. In this state, man takes the "leap". His
leap lands him in sin. Sin creates guilt. Guilt creates remorse. Once again anxiety builds up and increas-
es and a choice is necessitated. At this point, man
may take the leap faith-fully into accepting God's
plan for his life, or he may take the step of despair
into increased alienation and, what Kierkegaard calls,
"shut-up-ness" and eventually into a "demonical dread
of the good."

Kierkegaard has given us a perfect paradigm for
a Christian psychology. First, Kierkegaard has given
us a most penetrating insight into the nature of man,
This insightful portrayal of man's nature gives us a
real handle on what ails man and the way out of man's
ailment. From a Christian point of view and our explication of Christian psychology, Christ becomes
the model for man.

For me, I have no difficulty whatsoever in af-
firming that Christ is divine. I came to this as an
experience of a theological doctrine, not as a sub-
mission to theological dogma. I took His invitation
seriously to follow Him. My conclusion, personally,
is that He can be no other than the Son of God.
This point is non-debatable.

120

If you have never tasted a mango, it is pointless for me to argue with you about how it tastes. Moreover, all the ways in which I can describe its taste to you still does not give you that sweet, luscious taste. And when you do taste it, your uniqueness may speak of things I cannot know. But it all hinges on testing that mango. "Taste and see that the Lord is good" says an ancient manuscript. They that do, come to know. You see, the idea is strangely and strictly based on experiential grounds.

In my therapy, I too start with anxiety. I describe anxiety as the creative directive to be oneself in truth, relentlessly. I do not agree with the notions of neurotic and non-neuritic anxiety. I see all anxiety as creative. One may attempt to use anxiety neurotically, but this can only have the effect of increasing its intensity and thereby adding impetus for becoming authentic. This theme has been treated rather fully in my yet unpublished paper, The Message of Anxiety.[4]

Whrn anxiety builds up and a false choice is made in the direction of inauthenticity, the conscience flares and guilt ensues. Again, I see conscience as being at the heart of anxiety.[5]

Guilt also, in my view, is always authentic. This notion has received explication in another paper entitled Guilt and the Nature of the Self.[6] In this paper I noted that guilt is primarily the experience of discomfort that ensues from not willing to be oneself in truth. Guilt is not for things done or not done, but for unwillingness to be. There is no permanent resolution of guilt other than true self-affirmation in the fact of all and any odds. Does this resonate to the tone of the words: "Repent and bring forth fruits worthy of repentance"? (Luke 3:8)

Otherwise, the fruit from unresolved guilt is increased anxiety and increased insuthenticity. The Scripture talks about "sinning against the Holy Spirit" (Mark 3:29). I spoke earlier of man being spirit and of man as made in the image of God. Sinning, then, has a two-fold result: It is against the Holy Spirit of God, but it is no less against man himself. It is this process that leads in the last analysis to the despair of "shut-up-ness" and the "demonical dread of the good".

Psychologically, certain symptoms have been noted as persons seeking to avoid being authentic. In attempting to subvert authenticity, all kinds of physical and emotional problems have resulted. These psychosomatic or psychological problems have been placed in various categories, but relief has come only as a more authentic way of life has been chosen. Again, the discomfort of the symptoms have had only one objective, i.e. to point up the fact that man is on the wrong track. His pain and anxiety decreases as he returns to his authentic self. In my system of Christian psychology I see man and women as made in the image of God and as less than human until that image is restored.

Now, of course, we may be accused of setting psychology backwards into the Dark Ages of non-science, and of introducing values into a "science" that has extricated itself so assiduously from the tentacies of such vagaries. I want to suggest that, in fact, psychology has never been free from values. Let me continue to go out on a limb to suggest that (in my experience) the facilitation that takes place in the therapeutic task most predominantly derives from relationships. Belatedly we have become aware of this. No longer do we believe that the therapist and his/her value system is concealed from the patient.

Furthermore, the feat (sometimes called objectivity) that on principle precludes the therapist from giving any definitive advice or answers is, in my experience, poor therapy. When someone has lost his bearings and is going around in concentric or egocentric circles, he need, oftentimes, a word of direction. Nor is it being authentic to refrain from giving this lead. It is not sufficient to hide behind "non-directiveness". If a therapist knows enough to be a therapist, he ought to know enough to sufficiently understand the nature of persons and their deep essential spirituality and to direct them from time to time. I do not see how the psychotherapist can do less. Philosophies of life that are inadequate produce behavior that is less than adequate. This is as simple as the laws of cause and effect. To blur these issues until the client discovers them for himself may be too late.

In this attempt to explicate a Christian psychology I am aware of numerous limitations. Essentially, I have tried to show that psychology can only be truly psychological when the scientific approach is used as an adjunct. For more important than method, is the person. Indeed, it was the view of persons based on the procrustean bed of science that originally split psychology off from its natural domain of philosophy, and the distortions that followed have been responsible in very large part for misconstruing the meaning and nature of physical and psychological problems.

I have also attempted to point the way to integration. These are the formulations that I find both meaningful and highly effective in my own private practice. I sense no conflict in being Christian and doing therapy with religious or irreligious persons. Indeed, my respect and regard for the person is, I am certain, a most important therapeutic adjunct. Likewise I sense no conflict in being a Christian Psychologist, for my psychology fully incorporates the most vital meaning of persons. To lead people be fully human is to open the gates to the image of God in which they were created.

References

1. Finch J.C. Some evaluations of Freud's view of man from psycholoanalytical perspectives and some implications for a Christian anthropology. Unpublished doctoral dissertation, Drew University, Madison, New Jersey, 1958.

2. Hitt, W.D. To Models for man. American Psychologist 1969, 24(7).

3. Finch J.G. Christianity as insight. Insight, Winter, 1965.

4. Finch J.G. The message of anxiety. Paper delivered at the annual meeting of the American Ontoanalytic Association, Miami, Florida May 1969.

5. Ibid, p. 12.

6. Finch J.G. Guilt and the nature of the self. Unpublished paper, Tacoma, Washington, 1970.

At the time of this writing William H. Fitts
was Director of Research at the Dede Wallace Center
in Nashville, Tennessee. The Center provides mental
health services and consultation to the Greater
Nashville area. An active United Methodist layman,
Bill Fitts has consulted widely with church groups
and led many personal growth experiences for
Christians. He is best known as the foremost researcher on the self-concept, and the author of
The Tennessee Self Concept Scale. A clinical psychologist, he is at present in private practice.

Thoughts on How and Where to Find God
by
William H. Fitts

In the small West Tennessee town where I grew up, God, religion, Christianity and the church were very much a part of my life. If there were atheists, agnostics, or non-believers around, they were not known by those terms. Such non-Christian concepts and people were notable by their absence, as were representatives of the non-Christian religions, which were limited to one Jewish family in the community. My mother was a very devout Christian, and religious teaching was an important part of my home life. The churches were focal centers for social as well as religious activities. In addition, prayer, Bible reading and other religious emphases were also an integral part of the public schools and the other institutions around which the activities of the town were centered. Most of my secondary activities—sports, Boy Scouts, high school band, etc. were connected with either home, school, or church. All of them were heavily flavored by Christian teaching.

All of this is to say that my early life in a small country town within the Southern "Bible belt" had very different emphases and concepts than my present world of psychology. Even terms like 'psychologist' 'mental health' and 'behavioral science' were relatively unknown and unused. When I stop now to look back (something I rarely do), my present world at first appears quite different from the simple town world where my life began. However, further consideration suggests that there has been a rather natural and steady transition. My present scientific and professional activities are not really so foreign to the central aspects of my youth. Perhaps I can clarify this further, but first let me describe my present activities and how they have evolved.

I am a clinical psychologist who has succeeded in combining human service and scientific research. This is a combination that many others find difficult, since service and research often seem imcompatible. I find it particularly rewarding to be able to blend these two activities. Again, when I look back

125

I can see that my professional career has also
involved a steady transition and progression to the
broader scope and more significant goals of my present
work.

Psychology in the Air Force

After some limited exposure to psychology and
social science as a business administration major in
college, I worked for a few months in an accounting
job. This was interrupted by four years of service
in World War II. I was assigned to the Air Force
psychology program. Here I had a series of experiences which all seem to fit into a broader pattern,
i.e. society's attempts to utilize behavioral science
in the solution of critical problems. First I participated in the selection and classification of aviation
cadets for training as aircrew members. After the war
I worked as a counselor in the Veterans Administration
Rehabilitation Program. My goal was to help returning
veterans, many severely disabled, to find a significant place in civilian life. Next a detour through
graduate school provided new insights and conceptual
framework for a profession of helping others. During
this time I also participated in another growing movement within psychology--the provision of counseling
services for college students as a means of helping
them clarify their goals and directions for the future.

Tennessee Self Concept Scale

My concerns were broadening--from aviation cadets
to disabled vetrans, to college students of all kinds.
The goals were expanding--from selecting people to do
a particular job, to assisting veterans with their
immediate life adjustment, to helping people plan
their future lives. Through training and involvement in research I was also progressing from a phase
of knowledge acquisition to an emphasis on developing
new knowledge through scientific inquiry. My doctoral research, on the role of the self-concept in
social perception, convinced me that one's image of
oneself is an important variable in human behavior.
This conviction continued through my first post-
doctoral position as a research psychologist with
the Tennessee Department of Mental Health. During this
period the Tennessee Self Concept Scale (Fitts,
1965a) was first developed and a long term self concept research program was initiated.

126

Shortly thereafter another goal was adopted when I began work as a clinical psychologist in a community mental health center. This work entailed involvement with people of all kinds who were struggling with all of the varied problems of living. It was very rewarding to me, and seemed to be a particularly relevant way to translate Christian faith into professional activity. Again I was part of a nationwide movement to utilize professional skills and scientific knowledge for the betterment of man. I still believe that the practice of psychotherapy embodies the very essence of Christianity as taught and modeled by Christ Himself. An attempt was made to share some of the meanings of the therapy experience, both to me and my clients, in an earlier publication, The Experience of Psychotherapy: What it's Like for Client And Therapist (Fitts, 1965b). This work helped me to point up the essential ingredients in human relation. These ingredients are essential if persons are to achieve their God-given potentialities. I spelled these out as "faith, caring, understanding, acceptance, sincerity, and limits. The significance of these conclusions was emphasized in some closing comments:

This is what I have learned from psychotherapy. In my opinion mankind will not change radically until these essentials are found in many places besides the office of a psychotherapist. To me, the great challenge of this age is not the atom, or the other planets, or winning the next war. The greatest challenge of all is for man to come to terms with man. Somehow, through religion, education, true democracy, or psychotherapy man must learn to live with himself. I believe that what we have learned from psychotherapy is a big step in this direction. But specifically what can we do. We can't believe in people, or like them, or really accept them, just by deciding to do this. These are not attitudes or feelings we can turn on and off at will. But there are two things we can do. We can try to be honest, sincere, and genuine both with ourselves and with others, and we can try to really understand others . . . When we accomplish these feelings also, then we see that they change and grow too, and then our faith and

127

confidence in people begins to grow also. We can make a difference in this world, and when we begin to realize this, we find that we have also made a difference in ourselves. Life can be extremely rewarding.

In thinking about these things while and since writing these comments, several other insights have emerged more clearly: (a) it is very easy to translate my concepts of psychotherapy and human relations into the framework of Christian faith and practice; (b) Jesus Christ was the world's greatest therapist in that he not only facilitated miraculous changes in other people but also exemplified these therapeutic ingredients in his own life as no one else has ever done; (c) the world would indeed be a different place if people really put Christian principles or good therapy principles into operational practice; and (d) love or caring, acceptance, faith and trust (essential ingredients of therapy, human relations, and Christian living) cannot be "turned on" by simple acts of will—they must somehow be generated or learned through other behaviors. Such thoughts and insights have exerted a strong influence on my subsequent and present activities.

1965 -- A Year to be Remembered

The year 1965 was a significant one for me in several ways. The two publications mentioned above were both accomplished during that year. Each represented a kind of culmination of long-pursued avenues as therapist and researcher. However, the most significant event of that year was the sudden death of my brother, Dr. Paul M. Fitts, who was a brilliant psychologist and a truly outstanding person. His death was a terrible personal and emotional blow to me. In addition, it caused me to reexamine my own life with particular attention to my real values and goals in life. I began to realize that I wanted to make a larger contribution, to have a broader impact, as he had done. It became clear to me that helping a few individuals would never alter the overall state of man in this troubled world. As a result, another small publication (Fitts, 1965c) spelled out a broad research program which is still actively underway.

This research program concerns the self-concept and human behavior and it has proliferated into many facets of life. It has demonstrated that the

individual's self concept is a significant variable
in his/her approach to life, his/her state of mental
health, and many aspects of his/her behavior. As
these conclusions have become apparent, a corollary
conclusion has become more cogent: That the critical
issues for both behavioral science and Christianity
is the question of how persons can change.

     Thus my research has led me back to the same
issue with which I have always struggled as a therapist. Or perhaps it is the other way around; that my
insights and concerns as a therapist have influenced
the directions of my research. At any rate, both
activities raise the same questions for me: How can
persons change and improve their self-concept, their
behavior, their mental health or the quality of their
Christian living? The present state of man and
society cries out for answers and action. Yet the best
efforts of all the religions, of democracy, communism,
and dictatorships, of science and of humanism have not
changed the basic state of man. Man still does not
love (or trust) God, his neighbor, or himself. As a
result poverty, crime, riots, injustice, cruelty,
mental illness and other social ills still flourish.

The Primary Question of Today

     Raising questions and answering them are two very
different things. Nevertheless, clarification of the
questions is always essential in the provess of finding answers. To me the primary question of our time
is: How can persons actualize their full human potential? From the framework of Christianity the question
might be stated in other terms: How can persons become more Christlike, or God-like, or how can persons
get closer to God? To me, they are all the same
question. I believe this because I believe that the
human potential surpasses the potential of animals
in more areas than just intelligence. Man has often
demonstrated an enormous potential for love and compassion, forgiveness and concern, understanding and
trust which, when fully actualized, do acquire a God-
like quality. For me these qualities characterize
God, and persons at their best can be more God-like.
If all persons, more persons, or even some persons
could be facilitated in this kind of growth, the
world would be a better place and the state of human
affairs would be much improved.

129

I have differentiated this not only as the primary question for mankind but also as my own primary
question and goal. I have devoted much thought and
energy to this question in recent years. One product
of this enterprise is a recent publication entitled
Interpersonal Competence: The Wheel Model (Fitts, 1970).
I make no pretense at the final answers to such profound questions, but O do believe that the focus on
human relations which this work takes is a relevant
beginning. Perhaps a quote from that work will
illustrate the point and also summarize my own position:

> My personal religion holds that whatever
> else God is, He is the good in people;
> that wherever else He is, He resides in
> people; and that if I do not find Him in
> people, I may not find Him anywhere.

This position is clearly different from that of a
client who once made this comment: "I sure wish I could
get right with God; then I could just tell all these
damned people to go to hell!"

I believe that when persons can come to terms
with either themselves, their fellow persons, or with
God, they progress toward the fulfillment of their
human potentialities. I do not believe, however, that
persons can come to terms with God without coming to
terms with themselves and with other people. And as
Culbert (1968) conveys with his apt sub-title, "It
takes two to see one", I believe that persons cannot
come to terms with themselves in a vacuum; they must
do so in interactions and relationships with others.
Thus, to me, interpersonal relationships provide the
primary route to change, to self-actualization, and
to God. One of my chief concerns now is the search
for ways and means of improving that route.

I Believe in the Church

I still believe in, and am active in, the church,
but I must confess that I question the traditional
position and practices of the church on various matters. As a scientist I am less concerned with people's
beliefs than with their behavior. Yet I have listened
to untold sermons where the effort was to exhort, persuade, teach, or convince people to believe something
rather than do something. On the contrary, I have
often felt pulled or stirred to do something but

without the something being specific at all. Often it would seem that I was being persuaded to love, to love God, or people, or Christ. But how does one suddenly start loving? I have long been convinced that love is good and that enough of it would transform the world; but that conviction does not give me love, or generate love, or even show me how to find it. More operational definitions and opportunities for learning new behavior would, in my opinion, accomplish more than inspired rhetoric or strong exhortation toward mystical changes. This position was recently stated in these terms:

> I also see another way in which the church is missing an opportunity to be a more powerful, self-actualizing source for individuals. There is too much talk and too little action. Like college courses in psychology, there is much study and discussion about behavior, but little opportunity to learn and practice new behavior. I have maintained throughout this work that the learning of new interpersonal behavior requires learning by doing. Sunday School lessons and sermons help people learn what they should do, and why, but they usually provide little opportunity to learn by doing. It is one thing to know that we should love our neighbors and forgive our enemies; it is something else to actually accomplish this through democratic involvement and open communication. I know that these things can be accomplished. I have seen it happen many times and it is, for me, an awesome, holy experience. When the God in two or more people is released to make contact with the God in each other, men are truly fulfilled and actualized. I wish that somehow churches provided more opportunities for this to occur. (Fitts, 1970, p.54)

In recent years I have participated in many of the awesome, holy experiences mentioned above. I have seen love, acceptance, faith and trust become so real and meaningful that I felt God's presence in a way that I seldom feel in church. These times have mainly occured in groups--T-groups, therapy groups, etc. These are the times when people really open themselves up and share themselves with each other in honest encounters. Love, compassion, tenderness and trust come alive so vividly that it is indeed awesome. This is when I see

131

that the God in people meets the God in other people
and is amplified as a result. The whole becomes much
greater than the sum of the parts and spills over onto
everyone present.

     The truly spiritual experiences I have shared in
groups represent for me the kind of end product which
the church advocates. However, even though these experiences involve real feelings and behavior instead
of vague comcepts of how we ought to be, their actual
accomplishment still seems rather magical and mystical
to some. Thus, even after seeing these goals materialize, I would still wonder how it came about. So I
ended up with the same basic questions I had so often
asked in church: How do you make it happen, where do
you start, what do you actually do?

Interpersonal Competence -- The Wheel Model

     These questions generated much thinking, observ-
ing, experimenting, and theorizing, all of which led
to the publication mentioned above: Interpersonal
Competence: The Wheel Model. In this work, interpersonal relationships are conceptualized as the vehicles which enable man to change, to progress, to move
toward self-actualization and to God. Each person in
a relationship is visualized as a wheel for this
vehicle. Most of the focus of this presentation is
on the wheels, based on the rationale that wheels have
a direct influence on vehicles and that individuals
can change themselves more readily than they can
change each other. The Wheel Model also assumes that
the key ingredients in good relationships are Caring,
Acceptance and Trust. This assumption, however,
brings us back to the same salient question: How can
persons generate a feeling of love, acceptance and
trust in themselves if they cannot simply turn it on
by an act of will?

     The Wheel Model provides, at least for me, some
answers to this question. First, however, let me
attempt a brief explanation of this model. If the
reader will visualize a wheel seen from the side,
then think of this wheel as divided vertically into
two equal halves. The right half is labeled "Offering
Self" and the left half is labeled "Seeking Self."
Most interpersonal behavior can be sorted into two
categories: what we offer to others and what we seek
from others. When these two categories are translated into the wheel model, it becomes apparent that
132

to have a very round or functional wheel one must offer
as much to others as one seeks from them. This should
have a familiar ring to most Christians as a variation
of the basic precept, "do unto others as you would have
them do unto you".

In the Wheel Model, a variation of the famous
"Golden Rule" constitutes another basic assumption in
the form of a "reciprocity principle". This principle
states that, in general, other people will respond to
us in accordance with what we offer them. That is,
understanding begets understanding, hostility begets
hostility, love begets love, etc. This kind of reciprocity does not apply to all people at all times and it
does not invariably have immediate application.
Nevertheless it does apply to most people over time if
it is continued and if the behavior is real or con-
gruent. This old, familiar, and simple principle is
actually quite profound in its implication. Most of
all it means that we do not have to be helpless, passive recipients of whatever crumbs life, other people,
or God deal out to us. We can do something ourselves!
And, it means that if we only would (or could) do
what the ministers and churches exhort us to do--that
is, love our neighbors as ourselves--then things
would be much better for us, as well as for other
people. Again, however, we are back to the question
of how: How do we proceed? How do we offer real
love to others if it must be real and if love is not
a feeling that can be called up upon command?

How Do We Offer Love?

The Wheel Model deals with this issue as follows:
First: interpersonal behavior is differentiated into
ten basic components--Involvement, Responsibility,
Freedom, Understanding, Openness, Caring, Acceptance,
Limits, Consistency, and Faith-Trust. Second, the
first seven of these components are visualized as
spokes of the wheel, the Limits are conceptualized as
the two ends of each spoke (minimum and maximum
limits), thus defining the hub and rim of the wheel.
Consistency is portrayed as the tire--firm but flex-
ible, and Faith Trust is the material of which the
wheel is made. Third, the wheel is so constructed
that in order to roll forward it must first move
through the Offering Self half of the wheel. Fourth,
a sequential order is posited for the seven spokes so
that, in order to get ot the last two spokes of Caring and Acceptance, the wheel must first proceed
through the first five spokes involvement, Respon-
133

sibility, Freedom, Understanding, and Openness.

This fourth feature of the wheel model is the key to the question we have been raising. The sequence of the spokes is based upon several considerations: First, the natural order in which the components tend to emerge in relationships (i.e. all relationships begin with some kind of involvement or contact); second, the extent to which the individual can directly control that aspect of his/her behavior (i.e. one can determine how responsible or open he/she can be, but not how much he/she loves); and third, the extent to which one component is dependent upon the preexistence of another (i.e. Caring about a specific individual requires some knowing or Understanding of that person, or Openness is facilitated by Freedom). This model proposes that if Caring and Acceptance are offered to others, we can then seek (and generally find) reciprocal responses from others. It also proposes that Caring and Acceptance can be generated by other behaviors even though they cannot be "turned on" directly. This is accomplished by a willingness to risk involvement with others, if it is democratic involvement where we offer ourselves as responsible but from individuals who are also willing to risk true communication--Understanding and Openness.

Interpersonal Communication Leads to Caring

Interpersonal Communication then becomes the route, the means, the handle by which we generate Caring. If communication is complete enough and is fully two-way (that is, if we offer both empathic Understanding and Openness), then Caring will follow. This is a bold proposition which many people do not buy. It is also such an important proposition that it warrants detailed consideration and exploration. I have attempted this elsewhere (Fitts, 1970) and space does not permit that kind of exposition here. Condensed to its essence, this proposition says that for people to truly care about each other, and for this Caring to become unconditional enough to constitute true Acceptance, they must first come to know each other--intimately, openly, and empathically. Even more important, this proposition also holds that when people do achieve this kind of communication, when they do come to know each other this fully, then they will care about each other. I have seen this demonstrated so many times. When people make the effort, and take the risks, to achieve complete open, two-way communication, caring occurs. When it happens

134

it is an awesome, holy event which feels like God has
been released to perform His wondrous work.

I am personally convinced that this is one of the
answers to the "how" question that keeps arising. I
believe that people can generate true feelings of love
and Caring; that when they do, these feelings are re-
ciprocated, amplified, and generalized to still other
people. I also believe that true Understanding of
others and true Openness with others are generators of
Caring for others. Understanding and Openness, however, are contingent upon involvement with others in
such a way that we assume the Responsibility for ourselves (which God has given us) and thus claim and
maintain the Freedom to be a separate, unique person
moving towards self-actualization.

As this "how" question is partially answered,
others arise. How can we best accomplish this kind of
interpersonal communication that generates Caring and
Acceptance? What experiences, skills, sale practice
opportunities, and instruction best facilitate such
growth and learning? How can churches go beyond con-
vincing people that they should care, to providing
opportunities for generating Caring? In terms of my
self-concept research, how can persons learn to love
themselves as well as (and perhaps in order to) love
their neighbor?

These are the kinds of questions I struggle with-
as a person, a Christian, a scientist and a professional helper. I am glad to be a part of an agency
like the Dede Wallace Center which seeks the answers
to such questions. I believe that there are vital
questions to all mankind and that all religions must,
and will ultimately, concentrate on such questions in
the future.

As I look back now, my life seems to have evolved into a rather clear, coherent pattern. My early
life, as it was lived with both parents, a brother
and a sister, was heavily flavored with Christian
teaching. The real essence of this learning was that
life, Christianity, and God are most explicit and
vital as expressed in people and their relationships.
People are important, and Christianity in operational
terms means respect and consideration for the rights,
dignity, value and feelings of others. It also means
love, but the answers as to how to get there are not
easy. Marriage, education, military service,

parenthood, scientific endeavor and professional
activity have not changed this central focus for me;
and in fact, have simply served to sharpen the focus.
God is where you find Him; I find Him in other people;
and I find it richly rewarding when I can assist
others toward similar discoveries.

REFERENCES

Culbert, S.A. The Interpersonal Process of self-dis-
    closure: It takes two to see one. New York:
    Renaissance Editions, Inc., 1968.

Fitts, W.H. The Tennessee Self-Concept Scale.
    Nashville: Counselor Recordinga and Tests, 1965.
    (a)

Fitts, W.H. The experience of psychotherapy: What
    It's like for client and therapist.
    Van Nostrand Co., 1965. (b)

Fitts, W.H. The self-concept and human behavior. Dede
    Wallace Center (Formerly Nashville Mental Health
    Center) Research Bulletin #1, Nashville, Tennessee
    1965. (c)

Fitts, W.H. Interpersonal competence: The Wheel model.
    Nashville: Counselor Recordings & Tests, 1970.

VI.

THE CHRISTIAN FAITH AND BEHAVIORISM

Without question, behaviorism is one of the dominant influences in psychology today. Although J.B. Watson populatized the movement with his writing in the 1920's, the roots of behaviorism lie in British Associationist thinking dating back two or more centuries. Much of what educational and learning theory psychologists talk about it grounded in this point of view which emphasizes the importance of experience and reinforcement.

Many of the behaviorists have been agnostics and active atheists. It has sometimes been presumed that a behavioristic orientation and religious faith could not go together because the behaviorists seem so facile at explaining everything in terms of past experience.

Drs. Hites and Clement are two religious psychologists who are convinced that they do not have to choose between their science and their faith. Dr. Hites is a Dean of Administration in a State University. He is specifically concerned with relating faith to scientific method and the philosophy of science. He writes about "stimulus-response" psychology and the problems of human freedom. Dr. Clement is a clinical psychologist with interests in helping children adjust and in assisting the church in becoming an effective organization.

These men illustrate yet another way that psychology and faith can be related.

Robert W. Hites has been a professor of
psychology and academic dean of church colleges for
many years. He was professor of psychology at
Birmingham-Southern and dean of Greensboro College.
He has had a special interest in the religious values
of college students and has published research in
that area. His book The Art of Becoming is a clear
relating of the psychology of learning to education.
Presently, he is the director of Admissions, University of North Carolina, Greensboro.

S-R PSYCHOLOGY AND CHRISTIAN FAITH
by
Robert W. Hites

There has been times in the history of men when
it seemed as if the passing of one generation encom-
passed several ages instead of only one. Such is the
time between my boyhood and the age in which I now
live. The midwest of small towns and firms and the
far-west of small towns and mountains and space contrast with the crowded suburbs and urban areas today.
The mind of that era was not unlike that of the mind
of this country in frontier days. Man trusted man and
life had meaning in terms of relationships with
friends, with what was right and good, and with goals
in which to invest one's life. There were problems,
but problems seemed easily definable and there were
preordained solutions to problems at hand.

Religion was an integral part of that age. The
analogies, stories and parables in the Bible had in-
stand meaning to a people living so close to plowing,
sowing, reaping and to stream, mountain and forest.
Though the midwesterner of that day may have been
guilty of seeing David, Amos and Christ in terms of
corn fields, meadows and brick streets in small towns
they were several ages closer to the Old and New
Testament stories than we are only one generation later.

A World of Change

World War II, television, urbanization, technology, and population explosion, a decade of affluence,
and the impact of new ways of understanding the physical world and man have intervened between that age
and this and have swept away the certainties of that
age.

It is in this age of change that I must live, and
it is with the problem of this age that I must grapple.
Change has brought challenges to my Christian beliefs.
These challenges have arisen in large part from the
change in perspective which must come to one who reads
and teaches contemporary psychology. It seems that
psychology is a powerful explanatory tool fit to take
over the realm of much of religion. But in living with
and examining the basic assumptions of psychology and
science, one finds that they are powerful in certain
realms of life, but not in others.

139

pleasure. But the concepts of psychology were to give me anxiety because they conflicted with basic assumptions of the Christian faith. The seeming logic and power of the scientific method, especially as presented by the logical positivists, was what attracted me. Here was a way to define problems and to come to grips with them. The experimental method seemed to be the only tool which could be used to understand man--how he learns, how he acts in groups, and even the causes of his mental illnesses.

But what place has Christian belief in all of this? Is there a use for religion when there are powerful means to understand and influence man's actions? Is not the idea of God an anachronism in a scientific age? These are the questions Christians have been struggling with for the past two centuries. Many have abandoned their faith for humanism or scientism.

Psychology and Christianity: Both Explain Life

The psychologist is particularly vulnerable to the clash between Christian beliefs and his profession because both purport to explain human behavior. Psychology, being a science, makes the same assumption as science, i.e. that everything, including human behavior can be explained by physical forces. There is no need to postulate forces outside the natural order to explain man's behavior, and man's behavior includes religious inspiration and action.

There is power for the changing of behavior in the methods of psychology. Look at the power of psychoanalytic ideas in the treatment of mental illness, the explanation of human personality and elucidation of historical trends. See also recent applications of reinforcement principles to programmed learning, teaching retarded and normal children, treating juvenile delinquency and the alleviation of mental illnesses.

It seems that psychology is a powerful explanatory tool fit to take over the realm of much of religion. But in living with and examining the basic assumptions of psychology and science, one finds that they are powerful in certain realms of life, but not in others.

140

The most difficult and critical task of the
Christian psychologist is reconciling contemporary
psychological beliefs with Christian beliefs. To say
that there are no conflicts between scientific beliefs, ways of thinking, and basic assumptions and
Christian beliefs is to minimize the problem. There
are conflicts, and these conflicts are especially
sharp in psychology because here we are dealing with
concepts about human beings, not inanimate objects or
forces. The picture of both God and man may be different in psychology than it is to religion.

Science Conflicts with Religion

There are several issues where psychology conflicts with religion. The first of these is a basic
assumption in science that all events can be explained on the basis of forces within the natural world,
i.e. there is no necessity to call for a god to explain anything human or non-human. This also elimina-
tes the idea that a god interferes with the working of
natural law. What can challenge the Christian beliefs
of students more fully than to eliminate the idea of
God.

A second conflict is between the idea that all
behavior is determined by forces set in motion in the
past and the idea that we as humans are truly free to
choose. In other words, past events and forces in the
present situation determine what we shall do, and
there is no personal choice. We are automatons, fleshy
computers, pulled this way and that by the forces of
which we are a part, but over which we have no control.
Determinism in one form or another is found in
Stimulus-Response, Gestalt, Organismic and Freudian
psychologies.

Many contemporary theologians, including several
who claim competence in psychology, are attracted by
writers of the psychoanalytic school. This is a complete turnabout from earlier days when Freud's teachings were rejected because of their polemics against
religion. How is it that a school of psychology so
anti-religious could be accepted by Christians? One
reason is that adversaries on both the religious and
psychoanalytic side have either passed away or mellow-
ed and that younger psychoanalysts and theologians
were not caught up in the battle. Psychoanalysis was

141

used by Freud (and is used by the inheritors of his method) both as a means of therapeutic treatment for the individual and as a theoretical structure for analyzing and understanding man in his culture. It is this latter part of it that attracts me. It also attracts many other psychologists and theologians.

Another reason why psychoanalytic writings attract persons involved in religion is that the writings are presented entirely in a literary form as opposed to the semi-mathematical form of writing in many other fields of psychology. Some literary critics have pointed out that writings by psychoanalysts, other psychologists and sociologists are replacing the novel as a vehicle promoting social change. These are written about the inner search of individuals for peace, freedom, dignity, involvement, relationship and meaningfulness and the forces within the contemporary world which prevents the attainment of such. They illuminate the great themes found in religious thought. These writings are within a logical framework which, in this day, seems reasonable and scientific. One can have his literature and his science all in one palatable meal. Since most theologians are literary or word-oriented rather than mathematically inclined, they choose the entirely verbal branch of psychology and ignore or rile against other, more experimentally inclined psychologists.

The danger of accepting the literary productions of the psychoanalytically inclined is that you may accept also the basic assumptions of psychoanalysis which, to this date, may be, at best, partially valid; and at worst, invalid. This is not to say that psychoanalytically oriented writings should be totally rejected. There are many valuable insights or hypotheses for testing in them. But the insights are of the same scientific standing as the insights in our great novels and dramas. They present or portray the problem, but do not explain or solve it.

A major criticism both of psychoanalytic writings (and of some psychiatrists or clinical psychologists of other views) is that they are not based upon sound scientific method. Observations are not controlled, and rigorous methods of collecting data are excluded.

142

One of the tasks of the scientist is to examine the basic assumptions of theories, the experimentation which purports to derive from and support the theories, and the match between the two. On the other hand, it is the task of the Christian to examine the total human venture, to predict the impact of the forces within the total social and physical environment upon the integrity and dignity of the individual. At the present time Stimulus-Response psychology will aid us in both of these tasks. I prefer to begin with the research of the Stimulus-Response psychologists and relate their findings and theories to the larger aspects of behavior because this is the psychological tradition in which I was nurtured.

Stimulus-Response Psychology

There is extensive criticism of S-R (Stimulus-Response) psychology today among theologians and psychologists alike. S-R psychologists are accused of thinking of man as a machine composed of innumerable small parts, of ignoring the aspects of man's behavior which make him human, of preaching a strict determinism which denies that man is free to act in his environment, of writing as if man can be controlled like a robot, and of ignoring the great problems faced by man in his contemporary world while working on better methods of training rats to press levers. To some extent all of these accusations are true, but when the critics are asked, "What is to be substituted in its place?" they respond more in generalities than in specific hypotheses which may be tested. The S-R psychologists have been more creative in adapting their views and research to their critics than vice-versa.

It is my opinion that American psychology will continue to be S-R oriented for some time to come. This does not mean that it will continue to do research in the same areas in the future as it does now. A look at the problems now handled within this framework, compared to what was done twenty-years ago, will convince one of its change and its expansion in viewpoint. It will continue to expand by incorporating the results of research from other fields and by projecting research into areas now explained by the verbal guesses of clinicians and psychoanalysts.

143

All of this has relevance to Christianity today because using the S-R framework will enable the Christian to be in touch with the greatest concentration of research, research results and theorizing in psychology. This research and theorizing is the source of many of the current changes in education and therapy. We ignore them to our own peril.

But how can the Christian work within a framework of research and theory that denies God, freedom for man or (putting it vice versa) speaks as if man were a mechanism completely controlled by internal and external psychical forces? This seems to deny the great imperatives of our religion: the ultimate worth of the individual under God, freedom, dignity, responsibility for others, and love.

A distinction must be made between the basis assumptions necessary for theories, hypotheses and experimentation, and those assumptions not necessary. When the S-R psychologists' assumptions which are necessary for the formulation of hypotheses to be tested by experimentation are examined, little can be noted that has to do with freedom, dignity and love. In fact the S-R psychologist is very reluctant to assume anything that cannot be related logically to his experimentation. Even in the discussion of his research, the psychologist is likely to be careful not to go much beyond his hypotheses and data except to point out future research which needs to be done.

One looks in vain in almost all psychological literature covering experiments or controlled observation for what most people believe are the basic issues of our time--freedom, the integrity of the individual, love, compassion, and so on and on. How is it that the psychologist doing research as he does can speak on the issues mentioned above? Surely these go beyond his data. When the S-R psychologist espouses extreme determinism, he is going far beyond the bounds of necessary assumptions. He is as surely in metaphysics as are theologians. What I am saying is that we do not have to use the metaphysical assumptions made by the S-R psychologists. We may use a different set of assumptions and not violate the assumptions necessary for experimentation and controlled observation.

144

The Christian Psychologist and S-R Psychology

The Christian psychologist can talk about freedom, love and God within the context of S-R psychology just as surely as the S-R psychologists who deny them. The Christian psychologists who are working within the assumptions of Freudian psychology have been doing this for several decades. There is a biological determination in Freudian psychology which Christian psychologists, psychiatrists and mental health workers choose to ignore. We can just as easily ignore the metaphysical assumptions in S-R psychology.

Another distinction which must be made in between what psychology as a science can do and what it cannot do. Psychology as a science can speak authoritatively only about that which it can measure. Psychology can measure what values a man has, to what extent he has them, and the relationship between values and other behaviors, but it cannot say that this value or that value is the most important. In this sense, science is neutral. It does not speak of better or worse, dignity and love. It describes the probability that certain situations are followed by other situations. It is the scientist who extrapolates these results of science into issues such as integrity, the individual, and God, or the denial of these, and when he does, he steps beyond the bounds of science into philosophy, ethics or religion.

The psychologist is a person and like all other persons he/she tries to use individual structures of knowledge to cover all contingencies. Most S-R psychologists extend their personal structures of knowledge to the whole of human behavior and values. This is their right and even obligation, but we must be careful to note where the psychologist steps beyond the bounds of his/her cata and theory and becomes a philosopher or social theorist. This social theorizing is important and it is here that the Christian psychologist can and should make his impact. He can use the information gained from research and the tools of thinking from psychology and the imperatives of Christianity to enlighten present problems and elucidate processes for reaching future goals.

145

Faith in Psychology

Many workers in religion put too great a faith
in psychology. The believe it can say authoritatively
what persons are and what they will become if science
can have its way. Man is an animal who has the drives
of other animals, but none of the controls given by
instinct. Persons controls are learned from the group
as are the processes by which man satisfies his drives.
Psychology has learned something about the frustration which arises from blocking or delaying drive
satisfaction. Psychology has learned provesses by
which man may more rationally examine man's behavior
as an individual and, to some extent, as a member of
a society, but it cannot say whether man ought to be
regarded as having dignity, or ought to be enslaved
or free, or to have any of the values that guide the
destinies of man. Psychology is knowledge, but it can
be used to free men or enslave them. What guides the
uses of psychology is outside of psychology itself.
I believe that the values implied in the message of
Jesus the Christ and the Holy Spirit must be the
guide for the application of all science, including
psychology. Our churches have often mistaken the
distinction between rational knowledge and the values
or goals implied in using these. Sometimes the uses
of new knowledge are to help the Christian realize
that the churches have strayed and forgotten their
mission. We live in such a time. But we should never
believe that psychology or any science can set goals
for us. The everlasting task of the church and each
Christian is to point ot the way for a truly abundant
life for man through the witness of Christ.

So, in my work as a Christian psychologist I am
an apologist for S-R psychology. I commend it to
religionists I know. But I encourage them to not put
their faith in psychology. Psychology, like all of
science, can only describe. It cannot say what should
be done or what is important. Our faith does that
for us.

CAN A CHRISTIAN BE A BEHAVIORIST?

By

Paul C. Clement

Paul C. Clement is one of the more well known
child clinical psychologists. In addition to having
been granted several research grants from the
National Institute of Mental Health, he has recently served a term of office as president of the
California State Psychological Association. He is
a diplomate in clinical psychology of the American
Board of Professional Psychology and Professor in
the Graduate School of Psychology at Fuller Theological Seminary.

Can A Christian Be A Behaviorist?

My intent is to outline the major life experiences which have contributed to my commitment to the
Christian faith and my choice of clinical psychology
as a career. Central in each experience was a person
or persons who stimulated me to think of ways to reduce human suffering and/or who translated the Gospel
into here-and-now behaviors.

Childhood

I grew up in a rural community, Alderwood Manor,
about twenty miles north of Seattle, Washington. We
owned five acres on which we grew our own fruit and
vegetables and raised our own beef, poultry and mis-
cellaneous live stock. Although I greatly enjoyed
growing up in the country, my childhood was filled
with many tensions, anxieties and family troubles.

My parents were not happy in their marriage, but
they stayed together for twenty-two years, finally
getting a divorce when I was seventeen years old. My
father was an iron worker and traveled a great deal
from one construction job to another. He was a com-
pulsive worker, rarely had any fun, had no close
friends and dealt with his inner tensions by period-
ically exploding at someone in the family.

As a child I did not understand that my father
wanted to be a good parent. I thought he hated me.
He seemed critical of everything I did, except for my

148

doing well academically. His infrequent praise for my
getting good grades, however, was very important to me.

Although he rarely attended church himself, he
encouraged me to attend Sunday School. Basic instruction in the Christian faith seemed important to him,
but he never modeled any religious behaviors for us.
I don't believe I ever heard my father pray or saw him
read the Bible.

Whereas my father was excessively harsh, my
mother was rather lax in "laying the law down." She
was very anxious and a chronic worrier. In her relationship with my father she played the role of
"underdog". Even when I was in early grade school, I
can recall thinking that she worried excessively and
suffered unnecessarily. On the other hand I longed to
be able to defend my mother from the verbal and physical
abusiveness of my father.

My mother also rarely attended church. As with my
father, however, she communicated her desire to see
that I attended Sunday School and received a basic
education in the Christian faith.

My maternal grandfather was the only grandparent
I ever knew. Although he died when I was eleven, he had
a profound impact on my concern with religious matters.
Whereas my father tended to be loud, harsh, and non-
supportive, my grandfather was quiet, gentle, and communicated a deep concern for my personal and spiritual
welfare. I usually only got to see him a couple of
times each year, but when we were together he spent a
great deal of time describing his relationship with
Jesus and what it had meant to his life. As a young
boy listening to this grandfather of whom I was so
found, his personal testimony had a great impact upon
me.

Being troubled by how unpredictable and unhappy
my home situation was, I was attracted to the predictable quality of the life described by my grandfather.
I think, too, that I was troubled by my own hostile
impulses and fantasies of destructiveness toward my
father.

From age nine to eighteen, I sat under the
ministry of Paul Roper, a very unusual man. He commun-

149

.icated a deep concern for the problems that plague
mankind, and respect for the uniqueness of each member
of his congregation. Rather than trying to force his
listeners to accept his own doctrinal stance, he shared his perspectives in the Bible, and Gospel, mankind
and the universe. He rarely preached a sermon without
at some point saying the following:

> This is how I see things at the present
> point in my life, based upon what I have
> experienced and read. But I would not want
> you to believe it just because the words
> come from my mouth. Go gather your own
> data and then decide for yourself what you
> believe to be.

Sitting under the ministry of Reverend Roper was
a freedom producing experience for me. I felt that he
was interested in me as a person. As a young boy growing up, he made real for me many of the "fruits of the
Spirit". Not only has he influenced my religious belief system, he has had an impact on my philosophy of
science as well.

During the few years prior to my entering adolescence, I struggled a great deal with questions such as
"Am I really saved? What does it mean to be a Christian", etc. Reverend Roper seemed to have a good working relationship with God and he always seemed to be reinforced my faith in God and His goodness. He encouraged me to take all the time I felt I needed to find
answers to my spiritual questions. For example, even
though I had made a profession of Faith in Christ when
I was eight or nine years old, I was not baptized until
I was sixteen. When I explicitly asked to be baptized,
Reverend Roper encouraged me to think about the various
models of baptism and then to make up my own mind as to
which form I should take, feeling that such a decision
should be made by the individual.

Adolescence

As I moved into adolescence, I became increasingly
concerned with evangelism. By the time I was a high
school sophomore, I was passionately evangelistic. I
felt a deep burden to testify about my Christian beliefs to my peers, but I often felt inadequate to do
so. In attending evangelistic meetings during

150

summer camps and Christian Endeavor (CE) conventions,
I became increasingly motivated to witness and save
souls. I experienced almost as much guilt over not
witnessing enough as I did over masturbation and my
sexual impulses. During the summer between my sophomore and junior years of high school, I learned of the
Young Life Campaign which was designed primarily to
present the gospel to unchurched high school students.
I felt that if I could arrange for a club to get started at my high school, many of my friends and fellow
students would then hear the gospel and "accept Christ
as their personal savior."

Throughout childhood, from roughly age six to
sixteen, my vocational plans had never varied; I planned to become a commercial airline pilot. At age sixteen, however, I switched plans and decided to spend
my life as an evangelist working with university students, either in this country or abroad.

Through Christian Endeavor in the Seattle area I
met two ministers, John Klebe and Ed Underhill, whom
I came to admire, love, and respect a great deal. In
several specific ways they "took me under their wings"
and mediated the love of Christ to me. Both of them
were graduates of Dallas Theological Seminary, and I
decided that, following college, I would like to attend seminary at Dallas.

College Years

I began my freshman year at Pepperdine College in
Los Angeles. During that year I was very active in
Inter-Varsity Christian Fellowship. My evangelical
passion probably reached its apex during this year. I
had decided on the following: First, I would transfer
in my sophomore year to the Far Eastern Institute at
the University of Washington and major in Japanese
language and culture while minoring in French. Further,
I would become a self-supported missionary to French
university students by becoming a professor of Japanese.

During the summer between my freshman and sophomore years I began gathering information about requirements for being a professor in a French state
university. I discovered one requirement was that I
would have to become a French citizen. When I got
this information, I took it as a sign from God

saying that I should not pursue the preceding plans.

At this juncture I decided to become a clinical psycgologist. I had always been interested in human behavior and was concerned with finding ways of reducing human suffering. I had seen both my sister and brother, as well as both of my parents, have much more unhappiness in their lives than seemed necessary, and hoped I could learn ways of helping alleviate the psychological and emotional problems which plague so many.

Period of Transition

During the same summer that I decided to become a psychologist, I met my wife-to-be, Katherine Majovski. Following one year of courtship, we were married in 1959. In the process of adjusting to marriage, I began to be less and less concerned with evangelism. This trend had not been planned by me, and it occurred very gradually. I still have the notes from a very evangelistic sermon I preached in my home church shortly before getting married. I don't think I could have preached the same sermon with equal zeal a year later.

In 1962 our first son was born. Our second son was born a little over a year later. Not many months after I received my Ph. D., our first and only daughter was born in November, 1965. The realities and responsibilites of being a father seemed to accelerate the process of switching the focus of my concern from evangelism and the saving of souls to raising a family and becoming a productive clinical psychologist.

Until I got married, I was introverted and soul searching. I think that it is appropriate to label my phase of development from eight to twenty as my "Introspective stage." From twenty to the present, I see myself as being in a "productive stage." The more deeply involved I have become in this productive stage, the less intense has been my passionate evangelistic spirit.

A change in my time perspective has occurred concurrently with advances into the productive stage. In my introspective years, I thought a great deal about the future, including eternity. I also spent some time reflecting on the past. Currently I spend little time thinking about the past or future. I am too busy living in the present.

152

Another change has been a lessening of tension
and anxieties and a strengthening of faith and basic
trust. At the same time, there has been a marked de-
cline in my interest in dogmatic theology.

A New Role

In my own personal growth and development, the
church had provided a long string of therapeutic experiences and persons. As I progressed through graduate school, I began to realize, however, that the
church is not therapeutic for all who cross its thres-
hold. I used to believe that the evangelical Christian was better adjusted psychologically than the non-
evangelical (Christian or otherwise). I was shocked
and deeply disturbed to discover that this belief has
not been substantiated by psychological research. In
general, specific theological beliefs do not seem to
be strongly related to emotional adjustment; but in
those studies which suggest a difference, the non-
evangelicals appear to function better than the
evangelicals.

As I have reflected upon the relationship between
psychology and theology, I have come to the perspective that Christianity does a good job of revealing
what ways people should behave and why they should do
so, but it does not make explicit how. Here is where
psychology comes in. I believe that I have found some
of the means to bring these goals into being through
the use of the behavioral technology of contemporary
psychology.

Psychology and theology are both concerned with
human behavior and the nature of persons. Because of
this common interest, these two disciplines would
seem to be natural bed fellows. Such has not been
the case on the American scene during most of the
twentieth century. Fortunately, some changes have
occurred in recent years suggesting a gradual movement toward increasing amounts of cooperation between
psychology and theology. One such change has been
the establishment of a Graduate School of Psychology
by Fuller Theological Seminary. In 1967 I was invited
to join the faculty of this school after two years as
psychologist with the UCLA School of Medicine and
Harbor General Hospital. The unofficial motto of our
school has become "integration of psychology and
theology in theory, and in practice."

153

Integration in Professional Practice

Where I am most "turned on" is in the area of the
practical integration of theology and psychology.
First of all, I am interested in training clinical
psychologists who will be bridges between psychology
and the church. Many of our students have come from
evangelical, conservative Protestant backgrounds. The
people who belong to such churches represent a unique
subculture within American society. This particular
subculture has been highly suspicious of the mental
health professions and has avoided coming for professional consultation. Much of this "paranoia" has been
due to the fact that the typical psychologist or
psychiatrist does not "speak the language" of these religious groups.

I want to train men and women who will be "bilin-
gual" in the sense that they can speak contemporary
psychology and Christian theology. They will be able
to move freely and comfortably in either psychological
or church circles. Since they will understand the what
and the why of the church, they will be able to help
clergy and laity find ways of meeting their goals (the
how). My desire is not to tell clergy and church leaders what they should do; rather, I want to help them to
help themselves accomplish what they would like to do.

To this latter end I devote a fair amount of my
time teaching, writing, and lecturing. I want to stim-
ulate psychologists to think of ways they can bring
their knowledge and methods to bear on the problems
faced by churches. I perceive several areas of applied
psychology to be of help in these problem areas. For
example, industrial and organizational psychologists
could help solve conflicts among members of a church
staff or congregation. Clinical and counseling psychologists could provide case consulation to pastoral
counselors. They could provide courses, seminars and
workshops in the church on a wide range of topics. They
could train and supervise lay counselors. They could
help individual churches or clusters of churches set
up a wide range of therapeutic services, e.g., a
counseling center, senior citizens center, a half-way
house for adult mental patients, a therapeutic nursery
school for disturbed children, etc. Community psychologists could perform a survey of a church's member-
ships and the surrounding community in order to
identify the needs which the church is not meeting.

154

School psychologists could help Sunday School teachers do a more effective job of teaching meaningful concepts in a stimulating way, and could also help teachers learn how to handle behavior problems of children in their classes, etc. Architectural psychologists might help design sanctuaries which are more conducive to meaningful worship experiences. The possibilities of applying psychology to solve various problems present in the church are great.

Psychology And The Church

I am excited when I think of the church as a sleeping giant which hws fantastic potential for delivering mental health services to almost every community, large or small, throughout the country. There are over three hundred twenty five thousand churches and temples in the United States with more than one hundred thirtv two million Americans enrolled as members. Unfortunately, most journal articles and books on clinical psychology and psychiatry have overlooked these human and physical resources.

Contrast these figures with the fact that two thousand community mental health centers will have been constructed by 1980. The federal government's share of the bill for these centers will not be less than one and a half billion dollars, if present funding patterns continue through the 1970's. Add to this the amount to be matched by individual states, counties and communities, and the total bill for building these centers will run to at least few billion dollars.

It does not make much sense to spend these billions of dollars on construction, when we have so many facilities already constructed in each community, namely, our churches and temples. Even if churches do not increase in number during the next ten years, the 1980 church-to-mental-health-center ratio will be one hundred sixty two to one. Since church buildings tend to stand vacant six days a week, I feel that it is important to find ways of capitalizing on these physical facilities.

There is one church or temple for every six hundred fifteen people in the U.S. If we have two thousand mental health centers in 1980, there will be approximately one center for every one hundred fifteen thousand people. One of the basic tenets of the

community mental health movement is that services
should be offered within ready access to everyone.
Developing mental health programs within churches
would seem to meet this tenet more completely than
stopping with the development of comprehensive community mental health centers serving over one hundred
thousand people each.

That the churches and temples should carry on
most of the functions planned for mental health centers
makes sense from the perspective of developmental
psychology. The church is the only major social institution which is designed to deal with the person
throughout his/her life span, from the cradle to the
grave. I am interested in working toward these ends.

My Work As A Child Clinical Psychologist

As a clinical child psychologist, a major share of
my time is spent in the treatment and prevention of
psychological problems of children. For the past five
years I have directed a research program on child
therapy. In general, I have been trying to develop,
test, and refine increasingly powerful procedures to
remove emotional and behavioral problems and to teach
adaptive ways of living to children.

A general strategy which I am currently following
is to find ways to teaching parents and teachers to be
therapists to their own children rather than using professional psychologists or psychiatrists. In addition,
another major focus of my clinical work and research is
developing ways of teaching a child's peers to be
therapeutic agents to the troubled child. The ultimate
approach is one in which the child is taught to be his
own therapist. I spend part of my time trying to discover ways in which a child can control and shape his
own behavior in more adaptive and gratifying directions.

One of my more gratifying activities has been the
development and supervision of a training program in
behavior modification principles and techniques for
parents of preschool children. The basic goals of the
program are:
(a) to increase the parents' competence in managing the
behavior problems of their offspring; (b) to emphasize
the prevention of major psychological problems in
children by training parents to teach their children
adaptive behaviors; and (c) to develop and test a

156

system of professional intervention that requires little professional time, that is inexpensive to the families using the service, and that capitalizes on the resources of the child's natural environment.

Training is provided by students from the Fuller Graduate School of Psychology in a workshop format to groups of up to ten mothers or up to six mother-father pairs. Local nursery schools are the major referral source; pediatricians rank second in number of referrals. The program is a community service project sponsored and funded by a local women's group.

How This All Hangs Together

Can a Christian be a behaviorist? In order to answer this question, the two key words need to be defined. Webster's New World Dictionary of the American Language defines "Christian" as "a person professing belief in Jesus as the Christ, or in the religion based on the teachings of Jesus." I so profess. By "behaviorist" I mean "a psychologist or other social scientist who believes that scientific psychology should limit itself to behaviors which can be observed and quantified." Some behaviorists have flatly denied that there are such things as the mind or soul. They deny the existence of any events which can not be observed. Such persons normally would hold to a strictly materialistic philosophy of man and the universe. However, it is possible to separate philosophical behaviorism from methodological behaviorism. Philosophical behaviorism takes a positive atheistic stance and flatly denies the existence of God and all supernatural events. Methodological behaviorism is aphilosophical. It is merely a set of procedures and tools for observing, measuring, and modifying behavior.

Most Christians who know something about psychology have failed to distinguish between behavioral tools and behavioral philosophy. This may be due to the fact that many psychologists have been both methodological and philosophical behaviorists. But there is certainly no logical reason why a man must hold both points of view.

B. F. Skinner is the best known of the contemporary behaviorists. He has developed a system for studying animal and human behavior which has come to be known as "the experimental analysis of behavior." This system

157

is closely identified with the concept of "operant conditioning." The essence of operant conditioning is that human behavior is controlled primarily by its consequences. A given behavior can have five possible consequences: (a) it can produce a positive reinforcer, i.e. a rewarding event; (b) it can produce an aversion event, a punishment; (c) it can turn off or lead to the removal of a positive reinforcer; (d) it can turn off an aversive event; and (e) it can fail to produce or remove any positive reinforcers or aversive events.

Skinner, his students, and many other psychologists have demonstrated that the most powerful and predictable way to get a desired behavior to occur more frequently is to follow its occurrence with a positive reinforcer (a) above. A second way to get a desired behavior to occur more frequently is to follow its occurrence with the removal of an aversive event condition (d) above which was happening just prior to the target behavior. This second way of strengthening a behavior is less efficient than the first method under most conditions. One of the reasons is that whenever aversive events occur, the person experiences various emotional reactions which may interfere with adaptive learning.

Although there are only two conditions (a) and (d) for making behaviors occur more often, there are three conditions (b), (c), and (e) designed to make the behaviors which produce them occur less frequently. Condition (b) has probably been the most often used throughout human history. Spankings, scoldings, fights, and wars are all based upon condition (b). Unfortunately, its results are the least predictable of the three deceleration procedures. Coercion and physical abuse are often a part of condition (b). Condition (c) and (e) involve the removal of positive events and no consequences at all, respectively. They both produce more predictable results than does condition (b).

Why all this discussion of the basics of Skinner's operant conditioning? Simple. Jesus discovered operant conditioning! From a psychological perspective, the genius of Jesus was that he understood the best way to get people to change their behavior was to reinforce them positively for doing desireable things, the ultimate reinforcer being the love of God. The love of one's Christian brothers and sisters provides more immediate reinforcement. Jesus discouraged the use of punishment condition (b) as a means of getting people to change their ways and accept His message.

For me, Christian love is one form of positive reinforcement. Jesus provided a model of a Person who
used positive consequences, rather than punishment, to
shape other's behavior. He was concerned that we might
learn to love one another and learn alternatives to
impulsive, destructive behavior.

Some people are offended by the fact that Skinner
developed his principles in the laboratory experimenting with rats and pigeons. Even after these principles
were confirmed through research on people, many individuals were uneasy about their application to human
psychology. They especially became concerned about the
ability of one human to control the behavior of another.
But control is going on all of the time. There is no
alternative to behavior being under someone's control.

What is exciting, however, is the realization that
human beings have been created with the power to become
the experimenter on their own behavior. A normal process of development is the acquisition of self-rein-
forcing and self-punishing behaviors. I believe
Jesus's teachings suggest that in the same way we should
use positive reinforcement in responding to others, we
should also use positive reinforcement in responding to
ourselves. The second great commandment, "Thou shalt
love thy neighbor as thyself", seems predicated on the
individual first loving himself, i.e. using positive
reinforcement on himself.

My basic position is that, although Jesus was not
a scientist nor did He use scientific methodology, the
methods of science are in no way incompatible with His
teachings. On the contrary, scientific psychology
seems to complement the gospel and to have the potential
for helping Christians live more closely to the model
which Jesus provided. Not only can a Christian be a
behaviorist, methodological behaviorism can help a person to be a better Christian.

VII.

AT THE DAILY WORK OF TREATMENT AND TRAINING

Christian psychologists can be found in unlikely
places. They are not always in church or at church.
They are where Christian businessmen, physicians,
salesmen, plumbers, etc. are found - i.e. at work.
They often work with people where they are - in hospitals, in schools, at work or at play.

The two psychologists who write in this section
are but examples of the many secular places where
psychologists go about their professions. Dr. Thompson
works in a state mental hospital while Dr. Sharp
directs a training program in achievement motivation.
In both cases these psychologists are firmly convinced
of the value of their tasks. Dr. Thompson sees himself
about the task of helping persons bring their physical,
emotional and spiritual beings together again. He
feels this is the best meaning of Atonement. Dr. Sharp
is greatly concerned with assisting persons in acquir-
ing the energy and the motivation to make something of
themselves. He has been very involved with helping
underachievers find a purpose for living. Although he
calls this a tent-making ministry (a la Paul) he yet
sees it directly and explicitly related to a Christian
calling.

This is one more illustration of what it means
to relate psychology and faith.

F. Fagan Thompson is the head of the Psychology
Department of Rusk State Hospital in Rusk, Texas. He
is an ordained United Methodist minister, as well as
a clinical psychologist. Long interested in Christian
education, hymnody and counseling, he has more recently become invested in psychological development
and brain damage in children. He combines long standing service to the church with involvement in community mental health.

At-One-Ment
by
F. Fagan Thompson

My first real confrontation with life came when
I was about sixteen. My Mother contracted a streptoc-
occue infection. The treatment of choice at that time
was drawing the infection with a needle or by incision.
For Mother's recovery I followed the teachings of the
day and prayed with all the confidence of a believer:
"If you pray believing, your prayer will be answered".

Even today my memory is clear in the joy and
thanksgiving I felt to God when Mother seemed to have
overcome the infection. But a change in the weather
caused her to contract pneumonia from which she quickly died. My joy turned to grief and then to rage. God
had not kept His promise. For months I would not attend church.

Over a period of time I went separately to the
ministers of the churches in our small town. They knew
me, I knew them. They were Southern Methodists, Presbyterian and Southern Baptist. They gave me no comfort,
each quoting in his way, "The Lord gave, the Lord
taketh away, blessed be the name of the Lord".

None of this satisfied me. So far as I was concerned, they had nothing for me; either by way of comfort emotionally, or, of understanding intellectually.

I finally returned to the church without enthusiasm.

The Scopes Trial

Sometime later, the great controversy over the
inspiration of the Scriptures and how the world began
became focused in the Scopes trial. The theologians and
ministers had much to say about God creating the world
by command. They roundly denounced those who questioned
the infallibility of the Scriptures.

I began to wonder if the ministers really knew
what they were talking about. Consequently, I saved my
money and, somewhat surreptitiously, enrolled in a
course in anthropology from Texas State University. I
am uncertain how I accomplished this since I was in
high school at the time. However, it came about.

I bought the recommended books, kept them hidden, and read them with avid interest. From them, I learned that, indeed, many ministers did not know what they were talking about. I also learned the importance of being open-minded to new information. The readings in anthropology were most stimulating experience and increased my desire to learn. This cherished possession was instilled in me by my mother when she taught me to read and started me in school.

Early College Years

After finishing high school, I hoped to go to a nearby church college which has since grown to become a university. My faith in religion was once again challenged by my failure of the entrance examination in Latin. Although my latin skills were not very good, a student of comparable ability was passed while I failed. The student was the daughter of the college President. I began to wonder just how effective religion was in the everyday conduct of people. If such favoritism represented religion, I would have non of it.

Fortunately, I was able to enroll in a church-related junior college where I passed Latin. During the third week of my second year my father called me home. Dad wanted to send a young man, the principal support of a widowed mother and younger brother, to training school for licesing as a contractor. It was important that the young man complete his licensing requirements within the year, and Dad did not have the money to send both of us to school at the same time.

A supportive Incident

Faced with self-support, I taught school for two years. During this time, I had decided to try to attend Vanderbilt University. This was a rather wild dream and I had no idea at all how it could be done.

I contacted the brother of a man I knew, a minister living in Nashville, Tennessee, where Vanderbilt is located. A visit to Nashville to talk with this man seemed important, but almost impossible for me to arrange. As it happened, a friend from Oklahoma asked me to sing at her wedding. While I was there, her father, a minister, asked me to lead the singing for a revival meeting near Nashville. While there, I

163

met the board of the Community House where the minister I wanted to meet lived. The board hired me to be director of the gymnasium for which I received seventy-five dollars a month and a room over the health clinic. It was then that I thought, "Maybe, after all, 'God does work in mysterious ways".

In addition to the gymnasium job, I soon found work in a church as a choir director and youth worker. This not only gave me money for schooling, but also began an eighteen year period of similar work in more than a dozen denominations. Intimate association with such stalwart men of God as Dr. W.F. Powell of the Baptist Church, Bishop Maxon of the Episcopal Church, Dr. Vance of the Presbyterian Church and Bishop Decell of the Methodist Church, afforded me a rare opportunity to experience contemporary religious teachings and observe active Christian living and witnessing. These experiences undoubtedly influenced me to enter the Vanderbilt School of Religion for advanced study.

A Man and Unpardonable Sin

There was another experience which may have influenced me to enter the School of Religion. While Director of the gymnasium of the Centenary institute, I took meals with the minister and his wife who lived next door. While awaiting the noon meal one day, I answered a knock at the parsonage door. A very agitated man was there to see the minister. Upon hearing that the minister was not home yet, the man insisted that we both kneel to pray on the porch, within a few feet of the busy street. He prayed loudly, long and fervently that God would save him from the unpardonable sin he had committed. It was a sex problem which, while not socially acceptable, did not seem to me, even then, a sin which was unforgiveable.

The man was unreconcilable. Later, he was taken to a mental hospital. The incident resulted in at least two long-time beliefs for me. One, prayer is not in itself a healing for mental illness; and, two, such an individual needs an additional kind of help. This help, I felt and still feel, should combine both theology and psychology. From this event, perhaps more than any other, I decided that I needed to study theology and psychology if I were to help persons with mental and religious problems.

164

A New Concept

The venerable Dean of the Vanderbilt School of Religion, in a class in theology, introduced me to a concept of atonement which I continue to find meaningful. Theologically, atonement is man's reconciliation to God after having transgressed the Covenant. This reconciliation of God and man is brought about by the redemptive life and death of Christ. According to the Dean, atonement may be explained more clearly by a single learning device called "paired associations". The Professor said, "Atonement means literally "at-one-ment", that is, this idea of reconciliation suggests many areas in which man as a sentient being needs atonement, or at-one-ment.

At-One-Ment With Human Nature

We need at-one-ment with human nature. For long, long years man regarded his body as an enemy. The modern attitude seems to disregard body needs and give free expression to body drives. Neither repression nor free expression reflect the congruence, the harmony, and the rightness that at-one-ment of naturally controlled body drives gives.

At-One-Ment With Physical Nature

We need at-one-ment with the world about us, the earth, the grass, the trees. We have learned so much how to control nature that we have almost forgotten how dependent upon nature we really are.

At-On-Ment With Ourselves

We need at-one-ment with ourselves; that is, with ourselves as self-centered beings. When we do not possess a sense of our own worth we cannot accept ourselves as children of God. Otherwise we are likely to try to prove our own worth by acts of external associations. That is, we seek a profitable marriage, success in business, prestigious associates. We seek to build up our self-esteem by doing what will impress others rather than recognizing our own self-worth.

At-one-ment with self is akin to self-acceptance or self-esteem. When we accept ourselves, we generally have little difficulty accepting and loving others.

165

One reason for counseling is that it may aid
people in the understanding of their own worth and the
concurrent right to be, to exist, to live. Understanding, integration, reconciliation with self, or at-one-
ment with self, does not, however, free us from conflicts and, therefore, from anxiety. The growing,
maturing person will continue to experience conflict
and anxiety. But at-one-ment in the sense used here
will release strength to meet the ordinary conflicts
and anxieties of life.

At-One-Ment Religiously

We need at-one-ment in a religious sense. Religion, in its broader sense, can enable us to appropriate values that transcend the insecurity of the
present. To the extent that we can become one with
the Spirit of the Universe, we become more comfortable
with ourselves and with our fellow persons. Incorporating this fundamental into our thinking will yield
security which the threats of the moment cannot easily
dissolve.

Atonement, as explained by my esteemed professor,
is a much larger concept. It includes at-one-ment with
physical nature, with our sentient salves, with others,
and with God. To achieve this objective and to aid
others to achieve it has been, for me, a continuing and
consuming desire.

Study Abroad

Before I completed the course work required for
a Bachelor of Divinity degree, I was given an opportunity to teach music in the Vanderbilt School of Religion.
The University gave me a stipend to study abroad.

I went to Edinburgh University Graduate Divinity
School in Scotland to study psychology as applied to
relition and the arts. The years there were spent in
intensive study with many hours in the Scottish Library and the British Museum. It was from Edinburgh
University that I received the Ph.D. in psychology.

Upon returning to the United States, I found that
the depression had wrought havoc with my plans for
teaching at Vanderbilt. I turned to music and the
parish ministry for which I was trained.

166

For about twenty years I was an active minister. This was an excellent opportunity to counsel distracted people, but the mechanics of the church took an increasing amount of time. Finally, I decided to return to school. I entered the U.S. Veterans' Administration training program and the graduate program of George Peabody College for Teachers. Almost five years of post-doctoral study at Peabody and Vanderbilt and training in various neuropsychiatric hospitals prepared me as a clinical and counseling psychologist.

This prolonged internship and scholastic work was done in the expectation of returning to a church as an associate pastor and counselor. Since no openings came, I remained with the VA for several years and then became a psychologist in private practice.

The years I spent as director of a group of specialists working with children and adults were interesting, challenging and satisfying.

As consultant to a state mental hospital, I became familiar with that population and their dire needs. I decided to accept the state hospital's invitation to work full time.

Present Involvement

As Chief Clinical Psychologist of a state mental hospital with nearly two thousand patients and a dozen associates, my work is divided into many activities. Religious life values may not be mentioned in daily interactions, yet with me, these values are ever present in my mind and my practice.

A few examples of these principles will reveal something of the scope and depth of my endeavors. Any day may present problems such as the following:

Fear

A young person is referred to me who fears failure in college. While this type of fear is common, it rarely causes hospitalization in a psychiatric hospital.

To be afraid is realistic. If a child does not know fear, he or she may burn hands on a hot stove, or play with snakes. On the other hand, false fear must be appraised realistically. As

167

individuals, we must attempt to discover what
is real or unreal, rational or irrational.

In the case of the young person mentioned above,
a vocational evaluation revealed that his vocational goal exceeded his abilities. He was shown
another possibility which he could master satisfactorily and which also suited his vocational
interests. As a result, he was soon discharged
from the hospital, confident that he could succeed.

Anxiety

Anxiety is more vague and diffuse than fear. It
is a feeling of uneasiness or foreboding.
Anxiety overwhelms with an apprehension of im-
pending danger. The possibility of accident,
illness, failure, economic disaster and war all
are all about us. These are realities of life.
Each normal individual must come to terms with
these pressures.

Prolonged anxiety causes our bodies to become
mobilized for emergency action without consequent activity. This may result in psychosomatic problems such as headaches, digestive
problems, the inability to perform daily work
and/or a wide variety of other possibilities.

Locating the cause of anxiety is often very
difficulty because of its generalized nature.
A clearer understanding of religious principles, a reappraisal of our value orientation,
and a different goal are among possibilities
for the treatment of anxiety.

Hostility

Hostility may stem from frustration, physical
impairment, interpersonal conflicts, or anything threatening to individual goals. To
escape feeling guilty, we are inclined to mask
our hostility. We might become hyper-critical,
nag, hold grudges, become cynical, gossip, or
be suspicious of others.

Hostility may be turned inward also. We might
get a peptic ulcer, over-indulge in eating or
drinking, and/or become depressed or self-
condemning.   168

The understanding and controlling of hostility is a major problem in living. Frustration,
disappointment, discourtesy, stress and exhaustion are all common to our life. We must learn to
cope with such pressures by accepting what we
cannot change. For instance, we must accept the
fact that not everyone is going to love us, nor
will we succeed in our every endeavor. Some
problem in hostility comes to this counselor
almost daily.

Guilt

Guilt which assumes there is no forgiveness is
self-defeating. In this morbid guilt, the trans-
gression is magnified bout of proportion. Such
thinking is immature, rigid and unrealistic. The
individual seeks punishment for his/her guilt. In
effect, he or she denies faith in God's redemptive forgiveness.

Recently a female patient was referred to me
who felt she had sinned against the Holy Spirit.
Reassurance is generally futile in aiding such
feelings of despair. I asked her to read certain
biblical passages referring to forgiveness, then
asked her if she believed that Bible--that Jesus
existed, and other relevant subjects. She was then
asked if she were a "special" person, ordained to
die. Slowly she came to realize the inappropriate-
ness of her thinking with accompanying diminution
of pathological feelings of guilt.

Grief

Grief is universal. I comes through the loss of
a person, a loved object with whom one is closely
identified. The bereaved feels that a part of
himself is lost, and in a real sense this is true.
A father may grieve over his son who has committed a crime; a divorce may be tragic for both parents and children; a person may be disfigured or
lose a limb in an accident; a natural phenomenon
may cause the loss of possessions.

When we are grieved, we need to express our
sorrow. We should attempt to work through our
grief by talking, crying, and really mourning in

169

whatever way comes naturally. Thus we slowly, but
surely, rearrange our life details in a new
pattern.

Repressed grief, complicated by guilt and depression, is very difficult to overcome. Such a
condition must be dealt with through the psychological needs of the grieved. To tell such persons that God is good may not be right for them.
It certainly does not satisfy my own thinking to
throw the blame on God. I recoil from the quotation "The Lord gave, the Lord taketh away,
blessed be the name of the Lord." These individuals need freedom to express their feelings and
to have moral and spiritual support as they try
to build a new life. Following grief, there are
occasions when a counselor need only allow the
patients to expres their grief. This, of itself,
is therapeutic and may be sufficient for gaining
emotional balance.

Psychological Activity

A wide variety of psychological problems confront
a counselor within a weekly schedule. For example, an
individual who was in group therapy prayed a daily
prayer of supplication because he feared he would fail
in his daily tasks if he did not pray. His rigidity was
apparent. Hopefully, he can be led to accept praise
from others as more acceptable than constant begging
from God.

Another example is that of a long-haired, barefoot youth of nineteen, who had been living with a girl
and was not very depressed, wanted to talk to me about
why the girl had suddenly left him. Talking with him
revealed that the girl could not accept his slothful-
ness--she wanted him to return to school and go to
work. The choice for him seemed apparent.

-- A colleague came in distress because of malicious
gossip regarding his marital conduct. He was assured
that correct conduct does not produce guilt.

-- A long-time mental patient was combative toward
other patients and attendants. The patient was so insensitive to pain that he pulled out his toenails and
fingernails. He could stand flat-footed and fall back-
ward on a concrete floor. His brain damage was extensive and he did not respond to medication. For him, a

170

program of behavior modification was formulated.

-- A Young woman mental patient of seventeen ran
away whenever given ground privileges. She was generally rebellious of authority. Talking with her revealed
that she resented her peer group since they did not
have the wide range of experience that she had had, i.e.
marriage, travel, a baby, sexual promiscuity, etc.. A
program of work for spending money and an opportunity
to care for aged patients (which she did well) was
arranged.

-- A Psychotic girl was found nude on the hospital
grounds. Her history revealed that she was a physical
education teacher. A plan was formulated for her to
teach dancing to a group of patients. Results were
dramatic.

-- An alcoholic man had suffered brain damage because of his drinking, but he was now sober. A retrain-
ing program for a vocation commensurate with his present intellectual functioning was devised.

These and similar problems are a continuous
challenge to the psychologist who is conscious of
his/her ethical, moral and religious principles, his/
her concern for other people, and his/her professional
training. Each new situation may be regarded as an
opportunity to aid people to better understand themselves and to help them to fulfillment, happiness, and
at-one-ment withthe Spirit of the Universe.

For me, to work with people toward such goals is
personal happiness, fulfillment and a sense of at-one-
ment with the Essence of life.

AMONG THE TENT-MAKERS

By

Billy B. Sharp

Billy B. Sharp is a Clinical Psychologist and Minister. He conducts a private practice as well as working in Business and Industry. He has served churches and worked with troubled youth. He has long been related to the W. Clement Stone Foundation in helping persons help themselves. He has lectured widely and is the author of several books.

Among the Tent-Makers

Paul was committed to his cause, and yet he remained a tent-maker, sustaining himself. Through his contacts as a tent-maker he knew what the common man was thinking. This assisted him in developing the life style and organizational structure that characterized him as one of the most effective Christian missionaries of all time.

In the last several years, I like Paul in a manner of speaking, have been among the tent-makers. Acts 18:3 tells of Paul sustaining himself through his trade as a tent-maker at the same time he was spreading the Gospel. I too have vocational directions other than the ministry, directions that involve education and psychology. This particular combination of vocational interests has qualified me for a position as the president of a vital and influential corporation.

It is a curious odyssey that led me to this position, and an even stranger, more curious set of circumstances seems to be moving me forward. A brief review of the past may serve to clarify this.

Texas Farming

My early years were spent in the cotton and cattle country of western Texas, a country of broad skies and clear, star-brilliant nights.

Trees were scant and sand storms were in abundance, frequently halting traffic and stunning cattle into aimless wandering. There was a fine and enriching beauty in this vast, seemingly unlimited environ, enough for any man's contentment in life. But it was not quite enough for me. For a variety of reasons, my personal needs were not being fulfilled. The real meaning of life was not making itself known to me there.

In those years, as I drove a tractor, ground feed and herded cattle, I had an enormous curiosity about life and its implications and possibilities. I experienced a yearning for something else, a different, possibly even richer, environ. The decision was

difficult. Choices seemed limited. There were no television programs and inappreciable radio broadcasting,
so that one's choices in the vast spectrum of life
were not particularly conditioned by events in the
rest of the world. In fact, from that strangely enlarged perspective in country where the sky and earth
alike seemed limitless, the world itself seemed small.
You could choose to be a rancher, farmer, teacher or
preacher and very little else. There were small businesses to go into, of course, but for me there seemed
to be no possibilities there. As I moved toward matur-
ity, following a path directed more by accident than
by choice, a pattern was formed, unknown to me,
through vital personal associations.

I felt a definite need to be of service to others
and saw two areas in which I could fulfill that need:
teaching and the ministry. Shortly before being graduated from college, I made a decision to teach. But
when I was graduated, the Korean war was raging and
whatever other decisions I might have made, the decision to enter the armed services was inevitable.

During my term in the army I gathered a number of
different experiences that changed my decision from the
direction of teaching to the ministry. This was a
difficult decision that involved several additional
years of study; I had no financial resources and limited academic aptitude. My awareness of my own deficienc-
ies was corroborated by the professors, but I stayed
with it, receiving a good deal of help, and eventually
satisfactorily completed my theological education.

My First Parish

My first parish was in New York State, in an area
blessed by natural beauty and pleasant, accommodating
people. There, in Chester, New York, I became acquainted with some of the realities of the ministry. For one
thing, hard work and commitment did not guarantee
success, neither for the parish nor myself. The parishioners were kind and tolerant, but I was personally
frustrated, and my dreams of seminary study did not
materialize. I diligently prepared what I looked upon
as relevant sermons, but recurrent personal problems
always faced me again on Monday. I would devote hours
to the teachers in the church's schools, exploring
their difficulties with the students and seeking
solutions. But the problems with the students persisted and some of them were involved in trouble with
174

the law. My evident inability to resolve some of these problems left me with a sense of inadequancy, and I felt I needed additional study in psychology to adapt to this kind of situation.

The parishioners' needs were psychological as well as spiritual. A mother, for example, who had a brain-damaged child, could not relate on an inter-personal basis; she did not know what to do educa-tionally. A young wife and mother, whose husband was having extra-marital affairs, did not know what to do. An elderly man deprived of his family was altogether lost in the declining years of his life. I had a very strong urge, a hunger, to help these people, but rec-ognized my own lack of preparation in psychological study.

Psychology at Columbia

To remedy this, I enrolled at Teacher's College, Columbia University, In New York City, to study psy-chology with a specialization in family relations. Once I had opened this door, lights glimmered in even other directions. I pursued some of these, continuing my curious personal odyssey. Among other involvements, I participated in progress at the National Psycholog-ical Association for Psycholanalysis and served par-ishes in the inner-city of Paterson, New Jersey and Nutley, New Jersey. In my churches I had known both great joys and great sorrows. But something was still lacking. I looked for it both inside and outside myself. Then, after serious and prolonged introspec-tion, I believed I had found it.

My talents were well-directed when I was working with young people. This was the kind of ministry that appealed to me. Now I was faced again with the ques-tion of a position, and a fortunate set of circum-stances placed me in contact with the Episcopal City Mission in St. Louis, Missouri.

This agency had a dual-functioning program. It operated a counseling service for teenagers, along with a caplaincy service for delinquents from the troubled homes of the city. The mission offered me a challenge and an opportunity; my dreams and visions of fulfillment were atain revitalized. I had confid-ence in my abilities. I had prepared myself to do an outstanding job.

175

Youth Work in St. Louis

In less than three months, however, I faced un-
expected problems. Even with my preparation, my
counseling produced only a few successes. It became
very clear that what I had learned in the works of
Frued and that of other prominent psychologists did
not really apply to 20th century inner-city problems.
The troubled young people would come to me for an
initial session and listen politely to my interpretations. They would even return for a second counseling session. But, invariably, the secretary had to
write a "No show" in the appointment book when the
third session came around. Now, I can't even justify
their having come back for a second session. They may
have merely thought that a professional like myself
had more to offer than what was expressed in the
initial session.

My hunger for efficacious service was again left
unsatisfied. There was a difference this time, of
course, because there were no graduate schools spec-
ializing in therapy for teenagers. I had learned one
thing, however, and that was that the young people
could learn from each other. The process was gradual,
but the final results made it worthwhile. I had
learned as well that there were things the youngsters
I counselled could teach me, and acting upon this
awareness, I found that I learned as much (if not more)
than I taught. It was not unusual for me to ask a teen-
ager his advice on how I might assist another teen-
ager. In doing this, I observed a very significant
change. The youth from whom I sought advice and
assistance invariably began to improve his own situation. This happened repeatedly, so that I camt to the
conclusion that individual sessions might be cur-
tailed and a group-activity encouraged. Through this
procedure, peers assisted each other. Today, eight
years later, this procedure (which I came upon through
an act of faith) is a well-established practice.

Peers Helping Peers

As a Methodist, I have questioned why small-
group meetings have faded from tradition. The prevail-
ing assumption seems to be that the spirit can be
delivered best through a professional vehicle. I
question this. Troubled teenagers across the country
have taught me that the spiritual and psychological
aspects of life are best conveyed by peers, when some
kind of behavior modification is appropriate and ex-

pected. This observation, stated as a concept, is: "Peers are influenced most by Peers." The truth and accuracy of the concept is particularly challenging to the organizational structure of the contemporary church.

This concept was significant for me. Still, it did not have as much influence on my theological perspective and beliefs as another discovery. The troubled youths who came to me seemed to feel very defeated about themselves, harboring poor self-images. As they assisted each other, their respective self-images improved. The more successful groups were those that discussed the positive aspects of life, helping each other toward the accomplishment of very real and very tangible goals. The significance of all of this did not focus for many months. Adn it was a curious incident that triggered my focus and understanding.

Our offices were located in an old building that had been originally designed for apartments. Different rooms had been converted to offices, but the bathroom remained essentially the same. It lacked a mirror.

Late one evening I saw a sixteen year old girl walk in with a mirror. It happened that she had pilfered it from a service station down the street. Questioned, she responded: "You need a mirror so that you can look at yourself as you get better."

There was a particularly sharp, though accidental, insight in this, and I pondered it until the clear lights of awareness brightened for me and the doors to another world seemed to fly open..

This young girl, this child, had brought me out of the dark myths of Calvinistic and Freudian determinism to a belief that Christ did come to fulfill the law, not do away with it, and that a person can change, truly and irrevocably.

The Reality of the Cross and the Resurrection.

It was a small beginning, but a sturdy plateau from which I rose to a new level of belief and a deep trust in God's goodness and persons' potential. Each of us sees the world from his own perspective, and this is particularly true in terms of historical events. But my own experiences radically altered my perception of the historical Jesus and the ever Christ. It was only when I saw beyond the profession- al ministry and the obsessive pigeonholing of psyO chology and I was able to accept the significance of the cross and the resurrection. I had to have a pos- itive perception before I could believe that it was unnecessary for man to atone for his own sins. It had been my inability to arrive at this positive perception that encouraged me to accept and work within a deterministic psychology. Once I accepted the reality of the cross and the resurrection, I knew that my life's direction was decided and my dedication assured. I knew that my wandering ogyssey would no longer be directionless.

In four years of intense associations with young people, my life had been touched in many ways, and altered far more than I realized. Repeatedly, help for the person being counselled came as a behavioral change. The word that might best pin- point this change was motivation. Each person was motivated to do something different. This was a new perception for me. In all of my years of study and experience, the emphasis had been in insight and understanding.

Motivation and the Modification of Behavior

I was watching an educational film one even- ing (The Strangest Secret) when I came to an impor- tant decision. I decided to gather as much infor- mation as I could about behavioral modification and motivation. Implementation of that decision wasn't easy. Resources were few, and most of them were out- side the professional disciplines. The information available was largely in the areas of advertising and sales. It occured to me that those who were most qualified to assist me in my work were not pro- fessionals in my field of endeavor. They were not really professionals in motivational and behavioral modification either, but they were students of the phenomenon. My task was to explore their field and become associated with them in one way or another. The best educators, I knew, were those who were do- ing what they wanted to be doing.

Sequently, a friend made it possible for me to meet W. Clement Stone, a successful insurance executive. I had thought about working with motiva- tional theory and Mr. Stone had been exploring the possibilities of integrating religion and psychology, within an industrial framework. As I talked with Mr. Stone, an immensely dynamic and charitable person, I learned that we shared a number of interests and goals. Fortuitously, I was able to join his company and work with him. My specific tasks were left undefined, and remain so to this day. But the situation had many advantages, and continues to generate constant creative tension within me. Mr. Stone, I presently realized, had many of the practical answers in the field of motivation, an area in which I wanted to complete a theoratical framework. A system of achievement motivation emerged. The system was first used as an entity at Kendall College, Evanston, Illinois. Since then literally thousands of people have participated in different forms of the program.

W. Clement Stone Foundation

Prior to the development of this system, I served with the W. Clement and Jesse V. Stone Foundation. The work of the foundation expended and the operational aspects enlarged. I was appointed Executive Director of the foundation and devoted four years to reviewing grant requests and evaluating programs. This activity brought me into contact with hundreds of people who were on the cutting edges of their endeavors. It broadened my understanding and encouraged me to accept dictums which Mr. Stone subscribed to and often repeated.

Mr. Stone believed that it was our obligation to recognize and accept the truth wherever we found it. Over and over again he cautioned that no one person or discipline had all the answers. I found this difficult to accept because I had been conditioned to believe that there is only one right answer, although it is an answer that may be selected from several possible choices. I reevaluated the church from many different perspectives. The Foundation's work was closely related to religious activities, of course, and people involved in every phase of religion walked through the Foundation's doors to expose their ideas in the hope of finding funds to support them. I can recall particular days when I would talk with a person who had strong convictions about faith healing, and listen in the next hour to someone whose views on the subject were absolutely opposite. The kind of exposure I experienced served to broaden my understanding, as well

179

as to raise many questions about my own traditional functioning.

During the course of my work with the Foundation and Mr. Stone's insurance company, I detected a problem of communication in our country, a critical problem that is not often recognized. The communication gap I refer to is between the for-profit and the not-for-profit worlds. Those who function in either one or the other of these worlds rarely understand how the other world thinks and makes decisions for action.

Pursuing this objective of promoting a unified effort toward understanding between the two worlds, I established, through the indispensable help of W. Clement Stone, a corporation dedicated to using the principles of motivation and behavioral change to best advantage. Our efforts are still somewhat embryonic but they are growing and expanding into functional application. We employ knowledge from a variety of areas: general systems theory, two-factor economic theory and program planning and budgeting. I anticipate transplanting some of the developed programs into the institutional church. This is a difficult but necessary task.

The contemporary church, for example, is confronted by problems that demand solutions from the outside. The solutions are not contained in any single discipline or organization. These solutions will require the assembly of pieces from many areas into a new holistic configuration. The church will be altered in some direction, and fortified in others.

The Church of the Future

My projection for the church in the next two to three decades includes some of the following changes:

1. House meetings will return and find new emphasis;
2. Several denominations will share one building within a community;
3. Central administration staffs will be much smaller;
4. Local control will continue to expand;
5. Ministers will be paid according to services rendered, just as doctors and attorneys in private practice are today;
6. Most services will be conducted by laymen;

7. Seminary education will be conducted primarily
   on the site where the minister will serve;
8. Ordination will be more a result of commitment
   than education or function;
9. The local church will have a much more vital
   role in the educational aspects of the
   community.

In terms of my own enlarged perspective, traditional disciplines--theology, psychology, etc.--are no
longer relevant classifications. It would be difficult
to distinguish between my functions as minister, psychologist, educator and businessman. I try to combine
the skills from each in order to accomplish sharply defined objectives. I now recognize that I have never
made a career decision based on whether I wanted to be
a minister or psychologist. The decision has always
been based on what I wanted to accomplish, and what was
needed for that accomplishment. There are times when
I have to take the role of minister, involving all of
my knowledge from that profession; at other times, my
knowledge of psychology is the dominant, determining
factor. But it is evident to me that I am now in a
position where all I have acquired in the ministry, in
psychology and counseling areas, and in business--all
of this combines to give me the respective channels
for solution of the problems I face every day.

I have found something that was lacking under
those broad Texas skies of my boyhood, something that
Paul too had found I have discovered--an awareness of
the truth that can be gained only through experience
with persons and God. This awareness will enable one
to serve both God and persons to the fullest. My
odyssey, my search, although different, continues.

COMMUNICATING FAITH IN PSYCHOTHERAPY

Very often the public thinks of Christian counseling when some one talks about psychologists who are religious. To be sure, the religious values of certain psychotherapists are an important distinction between them and other mental health workers. There are many psychologists who are secular in their orientation. Psychology has characteristically assumed a valueless point of view. Many psychologists are avowedly anti-religious. Since much of psychotherapy is the shafing of wisdom (or a way of life) it is not unreasonable to think that the faith of the counselor is an important dimension of the therapist's approach.

The two psychologists who write here are both practising psychotherapists. They spend a good part of their work life counseling people with troubles. They share in these chapters some of the explicit ways in which they relate their Christian faith to how they help people. Dr. Warren believes that the therapist can provide the conditions of grace in a manner much like the way in which the love of God was expressed in Christ. Dr. Tweedie proposes that mental health and faith go together. In fact, he suggests, the job of the counselor is not fully complete unless the person has found faith.

These are important issues for the Christian psychologist and engaging in psychotherapy is a further way in which psychology and faith can be related.

Neil Clark Warren is associate professor and Dean of the Graduate School of Psychology, Fuller Theological Seminary. He is an ordained Church of Christ minister and a clinical psychologists. In addition to a serious interest in the graduate education of clinical psychologists who are Christian, he has spoken and published widely in the areas of the Bible and emotions, attitudes toward death and client-centered therapy. He published (with Thomas A. Oden) a book entitled After Therapy What?

Psychologist and Christian -- Can a Man be Both?
by
Neil Clark Warren

I am intrigued by the importance of style. In psychotherapy, for instance, successful outcome is largely determined by the style with which a client participates in therapy--far less by the content which he or she and the therapist discuss.

Yes, style is an important theoretical concept. But more importantly, I am concerned about the style which you and I as reader and writer will develop and share together. The very nature of this essay makes our interaction crucial. The style with which we process this experience will determine the value of the enterprise for us both.

Our "processers" have been programmed by who we are and why we are sharing these moments (i.e. our motivations and expectations in reading and writing this chapter). It seems to me that two assumptions are reasonable in thinking about how the two of us happen to be encountering each other in these pages. First, we share a common interest in psychology. Perhaps we are both psychologists, or perhaps we share only a curiosity about persons and what psychology can contribute to our understanding of them. But psychology somehow draws us together. Second, I assume that Christianity is of some importance to us both. We may even share a commitment. And finally, we are both intrigued about the relationship of psychology and Christianity--or more precisely, of psychologists and Christians. We wonder whether one can be both.

With these assumptions in mind, let's proceed. For me, the task is "to state from my experience the interrelationship of my profession and my Christian faith." Your task is to listen, question, argue, agree, and even change. Our task is to meet one another, share a common experience and grow together. And both of us should remember that the style of our encounter is what matters most.

The Psychologist Part of Me

As a psychologist, I am teacher, researcher, clinician and consultant. My primary responsibility as a teacher is in the statistics-experimental psychology area. I sometimes speculate that I am the only person in the world who teaches statistics and experimental psychology in a theological seminary. But there are also courses in the psychology of religion, clinical psychology, the psychology of death, and the integration of psychology and theology.

As a researcher, I am primarily involved in the study of death. The major questions I pose for myself are: (a) How does one's approach to death influence one's approach to life? and (b) How does one's Christian faith shape one's understanding of and relationship to death? My goal is to grasp the biblical teaching on death, discover the most effective ways of transmitting this teaching, and learn to facilitate an individual's growth in processing his/her death experience with "Christian style".

Beyond these concerns about the subject of death, I am involved in the study of psychotherapy. Having experienced the fundamental importance of productive process in therapy, my interest since dissertation days has been to discover ways of helping clients learn to participate in the therapy experience to that their chances for positive outcome are maximized.

Finally, in the area of research, I have had opportunity to chair a number of dissertation committees and to supervise many master's projects. There is a quality to this involvement that is at once more demanding and more rewarding than anything else I do. To think with a student about worship, for instance, and to detect and refine the important issues is highly stimulating. Then to share in the development of a research design which focusses accurately on a specific issue, to spend days in the slippery task of data collection, finally to experience the excitement of hypothesis testing, and then to begin the long (sometimes agonizing) effort to communicate the findings—all of this involves creative teamwork and careful, hard-nosed specification.

More traditional clinical functioning is also a
basic part of my functioning as a psychologist. This
usually takes place in at least three contexts. First,
I see persons in individual and group psychotherapy.
Some are adults and some are children. Some are
quite secure and growth-oriented, while some are terribly distressed and empty. Some are highly motivated
to change and others are terribly mired in unproductive patterns and resistant to change.

Second, I help to supervise the clinical efforts
of several advanced graduate students. This usually
involves an hour of individual time each week for each
student and countless moments in the hallway quietly
discussing the latest developments in a difficult case.
Third, there are graduate students, some old but
mostly new, who need all the clinical help they can get
in a moment of indecision or fear or confusion. It
happens that I teach three courses in the first year of
a six year graduate program. I have opportunity to
develop a deep relationship with many new students and
to share in their exciting and sometimes painful growth
and development.

Finally, I am a consulting psychologist. For me,
consulation has occurred most frequently in a church
context--and recently that context has narrowed to a
single, local church. The overall goal is to make
the tools and insights of psychology available to the
church to be used in the accomplishment of its mission.
Relatively frequent telephone and luncheon conversations with the church's ministers about counseling
cases they are carrying, internal concerns over staff
functioning, program goals with particular groups,
etc., allow ample opportunity for the sharing of any
contributions psychology has to offer. A current
goal for this church is that every member will have
opportunity to receive training and to grow as a relating, caring, sharing member of the body of Christ.
The strategy was to begin with the ministers, move to
the lay leaders (elders, deacons, teachers), and
eventually reach every member. The first step has
been completed, and the second is in process. A
fifteen week, two hours per week training series was
held for the six men on the ministerial staff. The
training was didactic-experiential, and the goal was
to assist these men in developing styles of interpersonal relating characterized by non-possessive
warmth, accurate empathy, and genuineness.

186

A similar series of training sessions will soon be held for the lay leaders. In the meantime small groups are beginning to spring up throughout the church and will undoubtedly influence the churches life significantly.

The Christian Part of Me

All of what I have said relates to me as a psychologist. Let me briefly sketch the Christian side of who I am. Fundamentally influential in my religious history is the fact that I was born to parents who were deeply immersed in the Christian faith. My mother is a simple, loving, giving woman whose emphasis is far more intuitive than intellectual. She modeled sensitivity and caring, and she made a love for Jesus an authentic and perfectly natural experience. My father, on the other hand, has always been a model of intellectual search and commitment. In a way, he was born forty years too early. He possesses a keen mind and is incredibly articulate, but he was educated in Iowa country schools which expected and really only allowed for eight years of involvement. Excelling as a businessman, his mind has always focused almost compulsively on the study of Scripture and the work of the church. Attracted to the very conservative Church of Christ, largely because of his own heritage, he has spent much of his life torn by his strong identification with the intense biblical focus of this group and his frustration with their irrational claims of ex-clusive rightness" and their tendency to be angry and hurtful to all "others", including congregations and individuals of their own brotherhood.

These parents and this Church of Christ group have had a great deal to do with my basic understanding of Christ, Christianity, the church, Scripture, etc. While always in some conflict about the attitudes of the Church of Christ, I came to deeply appreciate their emphasis on the centrality of the Christian community for a believer's life. And, while never fully accepting certain "key teachings" of this particular group, a conservative, biblically based "Gospel Hymn" Christianity was woven into the fabric of my personality.

The influence of my father's strong and stable approach to the Christian life was especially felt during my early years. But when I decided to become

187

a minister while in college, I was responding to the persuasiveness of a Princeton Seminary graduate who challenged me to recognize my personal strengths, the call of the ministry, and what seemed to be an obvious match between the two. As minister to our congregation, he preached forcefully about a just but demanding Jesus who expects our best effort and sternly calls us to full obedience. He not only awakened me to the possibility of full-time Christian involvement, but he alone directed my attention to Princeton Seminary.

In some ways it was not until Princeton that I heard the Gospel as gift rather than demand. President John Mackay brought the heart of the New Testament alive for me. In the Church of Christ I had been mainly concerned with the correctness of the church's structure and the way to be saved. In college I had become deeply aware of the demands of the Gospel on my life. The Christian system seems now to have come to be backwards. For, as I say, it was not until seminary that I was able to understand Christ's death as incredibly significant to me. I began to see that my long struggle to win God's love was ultimtely fruitless. I was justified by an event separate from my productivity in a moment beyond my control.

But when you grow up inwardly convinced that your behavior is what wins acceptance, and when you have become helplessly entwined in a denominational structure in which correctness is preached as the only way to salvation, the Gospel has a difficult time reaching the center and changing you from the inside out. That process is still struggling to prevail in me. For me, it is a matter of experiencing myself as whole and complete and loveable because of Christ.

For ten years after seminary, even during a rigorous six year training program in clinical psychology, I strove to relate the Gospel and the centrality of self-worth as theoretical concepts and as personal truths and experiences. All of this "striving" took place in the context of the Church of Christ, and it tended to be in conflict with much that was central to that group's approach. But when I became convinced that the thrust of the New Testament primarily concerns the needs for persons to understand their worth and view themselves as prized and valued, and when I understood that the Christ event alone was powerful

188

enough to bring this about, my direction as a Christian and a psychologist began to take form rather rapidly.

So, in brief, the "Christian" facts are these. I am strongly attracted by and committed to Jesus Christ. The Christ event has, in reality, set me free from a miserable process of trying to produce my wholeness. I have not integrated that fact by a long way, but I am "being saved". And I have full confidence that the process of which I am part will lead relentlessly to a sense of completeness and meaningfulness.

Let me state in a somewhat less personal and perhaps better organized way the nature of my faith. I will try to be brief and clear.

The Nature of my Faith

The Scriptures point dramatically to God as the Organizing Principle. All creation was shaped and energized by this single, Master Intelligence. He created man and the secrets to man's meaning and purpose all reside in Him. He formed man fully capable of processing life and experience in a completely healthy way. One consequence of this processing was a deeply satisfying relationship for man with the Creating Genius Himself.

But the secrets were so simple they seemed naive. How could it be that God would always prove reliable in all crises in which man's creaturely welfare was at stake? How could persons be sure that God really loved them without some conditions for that love? Perhaps it would be safer after all to establish one's own ability to handle life for oneself; then God would not be so crucial. Anyway, was it fair to expect God to care so generously without proof of a person's loyalty and prior worth? And so response to God's gift became response for God's gift. This need to gain control over the process led to one complicating distortion after another until the secrets to the healthy process were hopelessly lost.

But in the genius of God's history, a man came on the scene who embodied the secrets of life and was able to transmit them powerfully in simple, earthshaking, symbolic events. His life was not effective enough to break through man's destructive patterns, but for

numerous reasons His death broke the tyranny under
which man had lived. The old secrets were rediscovered because of Him, and the original image was restored.
Persons now know what they would have to struggle for-
ever to accept: (a) that their salvation must come
from beyond themselves; (b) that only the Christ event
could provide the breakthrough they desperately needed;
(c) that the appropriation of that event required a
long, careful process in the fellowship of believers;
(d) that genuine power was presently available to
facilitate understanding of the Christ event and to
assist in the fusion of that event in the believer's
life; and (e) that growth toward wholeness was a
consequence of that process.

In the Bible, God's functions are carefully de-
finded and differentiated, and if one function is deem-
phasized, an understanding of who God is suffers. He
is the Ordering Creator, having established patterns
and laws. He is the Redeemer, fully cognizant of man's
condition and willing to penetrate history to reestablish the original purity and unity. And He is the
Sustainer and Facilitator, working steadily and powerfully to move His creation toward wholeness and completion.

Now let me share the results of my efforts to
integrate my faith and my major professional interests.

Integration of Faith and Profession: Dearh Research

It seems appropriate to consider research first.
I have a fundamental commitment to search for order.
I am equally committed to the task of ferreting out
the laws which relate to order. This is the focus of
my research. My basic question is always: "How do
persons relate most successfully to themselves, to
this or that event, to other persons, to God, etc.,
and how can these processes be maximized? The foundation for this research is my deep respect for creation.
There is something awe-inspiring about the natural
order when one penetrates it. Not only are the planets
perfectly placed around the stars and not only do the
genes do their work, though infinitesimally small,
but the psychological sphere also has been sculptured
with equal percision and intricacy. In a context in
which disorder seems characteristic, my faith is that
the natural process lies buried, sometimes beneath
many layers.

190

The layers have accumulated as a result of sin. And sometimes the only way to discover the original creation is to study those persons or events which have become relatively free of sinful process. Sometimes the direct revelation of Scripture is the only trustworthy indivator of when the creation strata has been reached.

Take, for instance, the question of how persons can relate most meaningfully to death. If one surveys a given population for meaningful death approaches, one readily recognizes that there are many approaches, but few, if any, meaningful ones. The vast majority of most populations will deny death's reality, and careful effort is made to dismiss it as a parameter of life. And so the constructive role that death can play is lost sight of, and the creative tensions which adds excitement and zest to life turns to neurotic tension, buried as to cause but devestating in effect.

Others become obsessed with death thoughts, and the result of preoccupation with death is similarly negative. Death obsession is virtually certain to lead to confusion and meaninglessness.

One might reason that in the general population there should be an approach to death somewhere between denial and preoccupation that would result in a maximum of benefit for life and a minimum amount of unpleasantness and anxiety. But I have become convinced that answers to death's questions come only with answers to life's questions. My further conviction is that, apart from the Christ event, life's most central questions remain unanswered. Only as persons encounter the radical revelation of their worth in Christ and integrate that revelation in their experience, can they become able to process the awfulness of death in a satisfactory way. And these are the persons I want to study--the "livers" who know how to deal with death because they have learned how to live courageously and meaningfully. In is out of this study that the crucial variables relating to death will become evident.

Integration of Faith and Profession: Clinical Work

As with my research, I attempt to integrate my faith and my clinical work. There are two aspects involved in most clinical situations:

191

(a) Problem detection and specification: and (b) intervention. The former is closely related to the research process we discussed earlier. On the basis of one's understanding of how healthy persons relate to life and themselves, one assesses a client's situation and problems and tries to ascertain where the current difficulty exists. Once the problem has been detected, the clinician generally seeks to isolate it and specify it more precisely. All of this detection, isolation, and specification is usually accompished through the use of various assessment procedures which are especially related to the clinician's theoretical approach. But the important point to recognize is that every clinician assesses "in relation to" a norm to which he or she is committed.

After detection and specification comes intervention. This involves an attempt on the therapist's part to interfere with the unproductive process and redirect it. This generally requires countless delicate moves on the part of the clinician. The ultimate objective, of course, is to reestablish healthy internal processes and a functional personality structure.

When I encounter a client who is involved in unproductive processes, my immediate concern is to understand what he or she is telling me about his/her distress on a level as deep as he/she wishes to go. In the process of understanding I try to communicate my appreciation of and warmth for him/her regardless of the feelings or thoughts this person shares with me. And through all of this I strive to be as freely and deeply myself as possible. If I cannot be genuine in the process, the experience may be more hurtful than helpful for the client. My goal is to establish a relationship with this person which will allow him/her to fully explore his/her own thoughts and feelings without fear of evaluation or censure. The objective is to communicate to the client an unconditional warmth, a willingness to involve myself in an attempt to understand, and a genuineness which allows him/her to trust our relationship.

Now, when I relate this clinical approach to my faith, it seems to me that they lock together at several critical points. First, as a clinician, I am primarily interested in the self-concept. It is my observation that persons who have come to recognize themselves for what they are, and to accept themselves,

are generally free from anxiety. Equally important,
they are able to choose the behaviors they will engage in rather than being driven toward one or more
unproductive behavioral patterns. But the clients I
typically see place countless conditions of worth on
themselves and invariably lack a genuine sense of
self-worth. Rather than responding to life from a
feeling of loveableness, they consistently strive to
meet their own conditions for feeling worthy and,
just as the Pharisees with their laws, they invariably fail.

At the center of my "clinical" faith, as well as
my "personal" faith is the doctrine of justification
by faith alone. It tells persons that they are deeply
and enduringly loved and approved, actually brought to
the place of sharing fully in the perfection and
glory of Christ Himself. And new life becomes possible
when persons place their faith in God's power to do a
miraculous work once more in them. No longer is it
reasonable for such persons to speak of their detach-
ment and alienation, of self-hate or unworthliness.
They are made worthy in Christ and need to be concep-
tually clear about this. They no longer need to prove
their worthiness to be saved; but rather recognize
this as both unnecessary and ultimately impossible.

A second point of integration involves the
dynamic which, beyond the insight involved in justification, makes dramatic, inner change possible. According to my faith, this process takes place as the Holy
Spirit consistently operates in the believer. The
objective is to help individual believers appropriate
and integrate the meaning of the Christ event for
their own lives in every moment of their experience.
This especially relates to the relationship the individual believer enjoys with himself, with life, with
other people, and with God.

It seems to me that psychotherapy can be a vital
part of the "justification-appropriation" process. If
clients are consistently met with warmth and understanding as they explore their inner worlds, they
have an opportunity to assess their thoughts and behaviors according to the individual value of those.
The constant, positive response from the therapist
helps them to become free from the conditions of
worth which have been placed on them and which they
have maintained. The therapist serves as a mediator

of grace, and clients become progressively better
able to experience acceptance of what they are, and
then to accept themselves. Then they can relate to
another person, for example, with a freedom they didn't
have before. No longer must they be defensive about
statements others make or imply about them. They have
become acceptable in a basic way, and are far less
vulnerable to any threatened non-acceptance from another. Their relationships will become better
characterized by openness and genuineness.

The critical point for me is that the people I
see are totally unable to become new again and experience the image in which they were born unless they
receive power from beyond themselves. The patterns
(call them sin or the products of sin or the state of
sin) in which they are caught cannot be changed by
their own initiatives. But does that power need to be
something more than the grace of Christ which can be
mediated by a therapist? This is a very difficult
question, especially when the therapist is an effective mediator, both in terms of technical competence
and by virtue of freely exhibiting the fruits of the
Spirit. Such a therapist, in my experience, can provide conditions such that a client can improve significantly. But I have become progressively more convinced that clients can achieve full psychological
health only when they have a therapist who can effectively mediate the grace of Jesus Christ, and when
they are introduced to the historical Jesus and helped
to understand the personal significance of this event
for them. Sometimes this latter aspect is very difficult to facilitate, but when it can be accomplished
in an appropriate and sensitive way, I am convinced
that it adds a significant dimension for the client.

Integration of Faith and Profession: Teaching

The third area of my functioning which I feel is
related to my faith is teaching. In a sense, this
area overlaps all the others. I am focusing in this
section on that teaching which is formally related to
courses and classrooms.

Teaching, it seems to me, is a highly complex
task, and it is easy in thinking about it to focus
only on the transmission of content. To be sure, if
some content is not transmitted, the result will be

unsatisfactory. But if content alone is transmitted, the consequences will be tragic, though these consequences are often overlooked.

As a general rule, I have become convinced that a student learns more from encountering the person of the teacher than for anything else. This I think is especially true where I teach. Classes are small (usually ten or less), and discussion is central. Rather than an endless recitation and learning of facts, my interest is in helping each student turn on to the subject and develop an interest born of some understanding of the material and some appreciation for and identification with my enthusiasm for the field. For instance, in experimental psychology, I am far less concerned about students mastering complex factorial designs and control procedures than I am about their succeeding in catching a spark of enthusiasm for research. The reward for a good teaching effort is not the students' development of a thorough cognitive grasp of the field or even their production of good master's or doctoral projects, but rather the spark of interest which ignites their involvement in research and motivates them long after graduation.

But how does all this relate to my faith? First, it seems to me that effective teaching will be an important part of ministry. In the field of psychology at least, when a student learns something which really matters, it will happen because of considerable personal involvement. And I am convinced that it is impossible to teach well without becoming involved with the learner quite intimately. It this be the case, to teach a person is to touch him/her crucially as a human being.

But I sense that I enjoy a closer connection between my work and my ministry than even this would indicate. In courses on the integration of psychology and theology, for instance, there are cognitive discussions which turn personal, and intellectual bantering which becomes existentially alive. To talk about the significance of justification by faith, whether in a classroom or a pulpit, is to minister the grace of God. The teaching I do provides numerous opportunities to reach out and help others "grow in grace".

195

Integration of Faith and Profession: Church Consultation

The final aspect of my functioning about which I wrote earlier has to do with church consultation. At the center of the church's life and mission is relationship. And it is to the building of therapeutic and productive relationships that I am committed as a psychologist. Thus, my own career focus clearly overlaps the church's primary concern, and it is here that I believe I can effectively contribute to the church and its growth.

The Bible teaches that the relationship of believer is essential. The body of Christ is to be characterized by deep relationships which refuse to allow for sham and superficiality. The church is to be a sharing, caring community in which the health of each member is the concern of every member. I believe the church is responsible for teaching its members how to be therapeutic. It is here that I have found psychology helpful.

From research in psychotherapy it has been determined that the most therapeutic relationships are characterized by three qualities: (a) accurate empathy, i.e. the listener correctly understands the speaker and transmits this understanding verbally; (b) non-possessive warmth--the listener communicates to the speaker a warmth unaffected by anything the speaker says or does; (c) genuineness and congruence-- the listener is open and honest.

Numerous research projects have demonstrated that when these qualities are present in a relationship, the results are extremely positive, and when these qualities are absent, deterioration often occurs.

So the task becomes one of helping individual members develop their abilities to relate in these ways. When this happens, the church comes alive at its core, and opportunities for outreach and evangelism are multiplied. As a matter of fact, groups in the church often appreciate being helped to develop a pattern in which moving out to the world both precedes and follows moving in on themselves. The strength of church groups is maximized when service follows fellowship, and "coming to know one another" happens on the heels of sharing the faith in a simple, open way with nonbelievers.

196

I have become increasingly convinced that the
hope of the world is in the "called out". And I am
equally sure that the hope of the church lies in its
ability to develop relationships which are alive and
vital between persons and themselves, between persons and their God, and between persons and their
brothers and sisters. Because psychology is fundamentally concerned with relationships, it stands in
an advantageous position to share its knowledge with
the church and thus become a constructive contributor
to the "world's hopegiver".

This search project on which I have taken you
represents my effort to discover and articulate the
interrelationships between my practice of psychology
and my Christian faith. For me, the writing of this
chapter has been a reminder of the challenge and a
source of encouragement to get on with the process of
being and becoming a psychologist-Christian.

PSYCHOLOGY, FAITH, AND VALUES:

A CHRISTIAN COMMENT

by

Donald F. Tweedie, Jr.

Donald F. Tweedie, Jr. is Professor in the
Graduate School of Psychology, Fuller Theological
Seminary. He is currently the president of the
Western Association of Christians for Psychological
Studies, a group of persons in the Western United
States committed to relating the Christian faith
to the social and behavioral sciences. He has
lectured widely and is well known for his volume
Logotherapy and the Christian faith. He is the
proponent of Covenant Counseling in marriage and
has also authored Sex and the Christian Life, and
The Christian and the Couch.

Psychology, Faith, and Values: A Christian Comment

A place to begin indicating my role as a Christian in psychology would be to tell how I became a psychologist.

Although I was born in Salem, Massachusetts, my boyhood and youth were spent on a potato farm in northern Maine. My ancestors on both sides of the family had been farmers for at least five generations. My mother's family dates back to colonial days. My father's ancestors had emigrated from Scotland by way of Nova Scotia three generations ago.

College life was not a part of the family culture. Only two relatives had ever completed college prior to World War II. My intention, after being mustered out of the army was to become a farmer. However, the farm I had wanted to purchase was not available at that time, so I decided to take advantage of the G I Bill for one year and entered the University of Maine in the fall of 1946. Little did I imagine that the embarking upon this one tentative year of study would change the whole direction of my life.

My Love for Academics

It was during this first year of college as an engineering student that my appetite was whetted for the academic life. Subsequently, for the last quarter century, the campus has been the primary focus of my living. In undergraduate studies, I took only two psychology courses--one was in personality theory and the other was in counseling. While these proved to be of some interest, it never really occurred to me at that time that psychology could be a vocational option. At college my lifestyle involved excessive drinking, gambling and generally irresponsible behavior.

Conversion

My conversion was a personally dramatic event which focalized in a decisive commitment to try the Christian life. This was precipitated by the reading

199

of a manuscript by Edward John Carnell, later published under the title Introduction to Christian
Apologetics (1948). Prior to reading this manuscript
I had presumed that the primary problem of Christian
commitment had to do with the disparate character of
faith and knowledge. I had presumed that faith was
either an existential attempt to believe what you
knew was not true (a minor variation of Soren Kierkegaard's idea of faith, although I had never heard of
Kierkegaard at that time) or at best, believing in
the absence of evidence. A statement in this manuscript caught my attention and changed my whole perspective with reference to the Christian faith as a
live option. Paraphrastically, the statement defined faith as a resting of the Mind in the suffici-
ency of the evidence. In the light of this comment,
it seemed to me that the Christian faith now cleared
the guardianship of my intelligence and reminded me
that fields of science also were faith options.
Mulling this over in my mind resulted in the determination to make an experimental assay into the Christian life.

In a remarkably short period of time I found my
whole being cognitively, emotionally, and volition-
ally experiencing a sort of transformation. Retro-
spectively, I have been able to gain an easy empathy
with some of the accounts of dramatic conversion experiences in William James' The Varieties of Religious
Experience (1905). There is a passage of Scripture in
one of Paul's letters to the church at Corinth which
seems to give an accurate theoretical ground for my
experience: "If any man be in Christ he is a new
creation, behold, old things are passed away, all
things are become new" (II Corinthians 5:17).

The end result of my Christian commitment has
been a steady confidence in the Scriptures as an
authoritative revelation, the validity of Christian
values for personal and professional living, and an
enduring interest in Biblical studies. This should
not be construed as supporing that there have been
no personal problems, negative feelings or interest
in critical problems, but rather that these have
been more or less superficial aspects of a generally
fulflling Christian faith. Some of my religious
experiences have been only marginally satisfying.
I confess that I would be rather surprised if I were
to see the fulfillment of many specific prayer
requests. Probably the practice of reading and

studying the Scriptures, more than any single factor
has contributed to a general consistency in my Christian style of life.

Seminary and Beyond

My initial interest in the Scriptures (which
ultimately led to my conversion) prompted me to aban-
don my engineering major at the University of Main
and enroll in Gordon College, a Christian institution
in Boston. Here I majored in Bible and philosophy.
I entered this new type of academic milieu and react-
ed with enthusiasm. By the time I had finished my
baccalaureate degree, I was no longer interested in
either engineering or "hard" science, and decided to
pursue a seminary education. I applied and was accepted by Fuller Theological Seminary and in the summer of
1950 I arrived in California.

It was in the beginning of the second year of my
graduate studies in theology and biblical languages
that my academic career took another radical shift.
This was occasioned by a rather acute clinical depression experienced by my wife, which necessitated a
geographical move back to the East Coast. I began a
serious reconsideration of my vocational goals. We
had planned on doing a certain type of missionary work
in Africa, but now this seemed obviated by the fragile
emotional health of my wife, plus the discovery that
our two-year old son had a profound hearing loss and
would need several years of special education.

After moving back to Boston I found myself am-
bivalent about whether to study Semitics (my studies
of Hebrew and Arabic had been personally very satisfying) or philosophy, for which I had a more general
background and understanding. One of my former professors had neglected to provide me with a letter of
introduction to the chairman of the Semitics Department at Harvard, so I proceeded with an interview
with the chairman of the Department of Philosophy at
Boston University, Edgar S. Brightman. I was greeted
with open arms in this department and given a very
good opportunity for study. An assistantship was
available and a waiver of a master's degree was
granted me in lieu of the graduate study I had already finished.

But my now historical philosophy and secular
history of ideas were pallid in comparison with
Christian apologetics and the general area of biblical studies for which I had an existential enthusiasm. The end result was that after the first semester of graduate study, I resigned the assistantship
and left for Main for the summer. By now I had developed an enthusiasm in the area of psychiatry.
This new direction was probably precipitated by the
concurrent emotional problems experienced by my wife.
I applied at the University of New Hampshire for the
fall semester in the School of Medicine.

An Invitation to Teach at Gordon

One week before I was due at the University, I
received an invitation to teach at my old alma mater,
Gordon College. Suddenly this seemed to be the will
of God for my life. We said goodbye to our families
in Maine, and along with our two sons and baggage,
drove to Boston.

Arrived at Gordon I discovered myself to be an
instructor in biblical theology, debate, and medieval
philosophy. The following year, I was to teach an
introductory course in psychology as well. I found
psychology an intriguing field of investigation for me.
Going back to Boston University where I had been studying philosophy the previous year, I resumed my candi-
dacy in the Philosophy Department and changed the
direction of my major interest to philosophical psychology. My decision was influenced, no doubt, by the
installation of a new chairman in this department who
had dual interests in philosophy and psychology. He
encouraged and supported my new perspective. His
appointment had occurred as a result of the sudden
critical illness and ensuing death of my major professor, Dr. Brightman. By now I was teaching half time
in the Psychology Department and half time in the
Philosophy Department at Gordon.

Most of my theoretical involvement at Boston
University was in existential psychology, particularly as it related to Soren Kierkegaard and Martin
Heidegger. My dissertation evolved as a theoretical
study of the significance of dread (Angst) in the
writings of these two men.

202

Vienna and Lexington

I took post doctoral studies in the psychology
of religion and a year of psychiatric studies at the
University of Vienna. The work in Vienna compensat-
ed in some measure for my rather meager formal involvement in the field of psychology in undergraduate
and graduate school days. The experience as a clinical associate in a neurological and psychotherapeutic
outpatient department was very rewarding. Here I was
able to channel some attitudes and interests, as well
as to accumulate experience which already had been
accuring through the task demands of student counseling on Gordon's campus. The exposure to a psychiart-
rist of Viktor Frankl's stature was invaluable. One
other significant involvement occurred two years later
when I received a government appointment to serve as
a research specialist for a year in a rather specialized area of study--phenomenological psychiatry. This
became an opportunity to work with Dr. Ewin Straus,
one of the world's foremost phenomenologists, at the
Veterans' Administration Hospital in Lexington, Ken-
tucky. Now my focus became an increasing specialization in phenomenological and existential psychiatry.
Having already written a theoretical dissertation in
the foundation aspect of this modern movement, and
having studied extensively with two of its leaders
(Frankl and Straus), I found existential psychology
becoming more and more my academic field.

By this rather circuitous route I became a
psychologist and became primarily occupied and preoccupied with clinical theory.

Fuller School of Psychology

My current academic involvement is as professor
of psychology at the Graduate School of Psychology
of Fuller Theological Seminary. I function rather
informally as professor of history of psychology and
philosophical psychology. I also teach the psychotherapeutic treatment of adults with special emphasis on marriage. I came here initially to establish
a community counseling center which would become a
research and training center for Fuller's new graduate school in clinical psychology, a novel attempt
to integrate the fields of psychology and theology.
Other academic responsibilities that relate to the

clinical functioning of our program include the
supervision of interns in psychotherapy, and the
guidance of master's level and doctoral level research projects.

In the academic curriculum at Fuller there are a
series of seminars called "integration seminars".
These are team taught by members of the faculty of the
School of Psychology and the School of Theology. By
turn, I participate in these. I also offer seminars in
the clinical application of hypnosis, and in marriage
and family counseling.

Psychology and Faith

A part of the assignment of this essay had to do
with an explication of the nature of my faith. The
most adequate characterization of my Christian commitment is to term it a biblical Christianity.

Probably more than men in any other field of study,
psychologists have been perceived as being irreligious.
This can be understood historically inasmuch as two of
the leading influences in the development of psychology,
Sigmund Freud and John Watson, both personally and
theoretically repudiated a religious view of life.

Traditionally, there has been a good deal of discussion in literature and in the classroom about the
incompatibility of a religious world view and the data
of psychology. I would contend that the two disciplines
theology and psychology, are just as scientific or
unscientific as the method by which they are observed
and categorized. However, they are interpreted always
as commitment beyond the facts, and are to that degree
a matter of faith. In studying the premises of both
disciplines, as well as those of philosophy, I am at a
loss to sense any essential tension. That is not to
say that there are no theoretical problems, but rather
that theoretical problems between psychology and the
Christian faith are no more difficult or theoretically
thorny than problems within either of the two disciplines. Instead of finding it necessary to compartmen-
talize these orders of experience, I have found them to
be mutually complementary. The study of psychology
has enhanced my commitment to the Christian faith, and
my study as a Christian has deepened my insight and
commitment to psychology.

204

In my judgment, the general precepts of Christianity are highly resourceful for the field in terms of understanding the emotional life. This is to perceive "bad feelings" from the viewpoint of the past, the future and the present. In general, I characterize these negative moods as states of dread. The dread of the past involves guilt feelings. The dread of the future involves anxiety. The present involves two modes of dread--anger and fear. Dread arises when there is a personal threat in one's environment. Anxiety and guilt feelings are more difficult to cope with because they relate to dimensions of experience which are beyond control. We are unable to "turn back the clock" or to re-enter the past. We are equally unable to turn the corner of the future. The reason these two concepts are so critical in the clinical area is because they relate to experiences that seem to defy the possibility of immediate action for change. The dreads of the present are less crippling emotionally because of the possibility of present action. Anger is a feeling state in which the threatening object in one's environment is to be destroyed. Under the moods of anger, our impulses are to attack what threatens. Fear motivates an impulse to flee from the apparent source of danger. While such a scheme is a bit arbitrary and perhaps an oversimplification, it covers the general conditions under which most persons report emotional illness. In the field of psychology, these foci of "bad feelings" have been the subject of many theoretical and experimental essays.

In my schematic outline, the desired "good feelings" that characterize a state of well-being may be seen in the same "phenomenology of time". For instance, the bad feelings of the past, guilt, are redeemed when there is a feeling of forgiveness. I call these positive moods the moods of joy. Forgiveness is the joy of the past. When anxiety, a catastrophic mood of threat from the future, is transmuted into a positive mood, then it may be called hope. The good moods of the present are love, as a redemption from anger' while faith is the counterpart to fear.

I do not know any value system or value commitment that so readily serves to transmute bad feelings into good feelings, dread into joy, as that which is found in Christ.

This has been true in my own life, and I have seen it frequently in the lives of others. In Christ we have the possibility of redeeming the past, vouchsafing the future, and a provision for personal joy and power in the present. It is my judgment that no other theories so well afford resources of positive mental health.

Should a Psychologist Impose Values?

This consideration points up a problem area that I would like to discuss: Should a psychotherapist impose his or her value systems upon persons who seek his/her aid?

There has been a tradition in clinical psychology that the therapist should be neutral in value judgments. It has been thought that he/she should not reflect his/her own personal values into the counseling situation but should merely reflect and clarify the values of the counselee as they arise in the context of the counseling. This is (at present) a shaky tradition, inasmuch as most of the evidence indicates that the values of the therapist will inevitably be involved. There is also an indication that the therapist's judgment of progress in therapy will be to a significant degree, based upon the proportions to which the patient identifies with the values of the therapist. The therapist will, no doubt, evaluate his/her effectiveness in terms of how well his/her own values are received by the patient. Apparently this is done largely on an implicit level from the viewpoint of the counselor. Thus the psychotherapist who offers professional service to help distressed persons find meaning for their lives, for weal or for woe, is perceived by his/her clientele as a dispenser of values for living.

A Christian counselor is in the same situation. The question seems to be not whether the counselor will influence the counseling process with his/her value system, but rather whether he/she will do it consciously or unconsciously. By default or by design, it will occur.

One often hears that it is inappropriate to impose values in psycholotherapy and I agree. However, my agreement is not based upon any particular questions of morality or ethics, but rather on the fact that it is next to impossible to successfully impose

206

one's values upon another. Such an attempt draws a
negative reaction. However, to expose one's value is
another matter. Sharing one's personal philosophy of
life and values at an appropriate time during the
course of therapy can be helpful. It would seem passing strange and a matter of questionable morality were
the therapist not to expose his values if he believed
that he had discovered some extremely important found-
ational factors for successful living.

Christian Psychotherapy?

This brings us to a point we should consider as
to whether it is valid to use the term "Christian" as
an adjectival modifier for psychotherapy. Some believe this would reduce the science of psychotherapy
to an absurdity. They insist that this reasoning
would imply that there is a special kind of procedure
a Christian should employ for every action, such as
Christian surgery, Christian anesthesia, or Christian
mechanics.

If this is their conclusion, then I suppose we
should make the most of it, for it certainly is to the
point. This radical approach is a central component
of Christianity. Christianity is radical--it penetrates to the radix, the root of everything. It maintains
that the God and Father of Jesus Christ is the Sover-
eign Controller and Creator of heaven and earth. Therefore, no vocation or vocational art is exempt from His
jurisdiction.

Every hypothesis, and each instance of hypothesis testing flows from a basic philosophy of life.
Each scientific observation is affected by the subjective experience and frame of reference of the
observer. Each subject taught is modified by the
philosophical perspective, whether conscious or unconscious, of the teacher. Every field of science is
relative to the philosophical foundation of the one
who articulates the field.

According to the Christian world-view, objectivity and stability in the world can be found only in
Christ. This premise implies the validity of using
such a term as "Christian psychotherapy".

The myth of neutrality and objectivity has been a common belief of psychotherapists. To the uninitiated, this seems to be a strange situation, for nothing would seem more obvious than that the individual with a mental disorder is having a serious value problem. That individual's value system, ethical ideals, moral standards and world view are all involved in his personal problem and there is much evidence to suppose that an unstable set of values is the real root of his illness. Many contemporary psychologists, both secular and religious, are now recognizing the necessity of re-evaluating the whole concept of values in psychotherapy. The recognition that value neutrality is an impossibility and that value change in the life of a person can be a positive goal, is becoming increasingly defended in recent literature. Thus, for the Christian who is a psychotherapist to reflect Christian values in a context of psychotherapy is not only desirable but also unavoidable.

The Christian therapist is neither exclusively passive nor authoritarian but, as many other therapists move in the dialectic of these two extremes, so must the Christian therapist. The subtle but significant difference between presenting values to the patient, and imposing them on the patient is extremely important. The Christian therapist, in suggesting value options, does not take away the patient's freedom, but rather encourages him/her to exercise it more responsibly. The patient's problem is often that he/she never learned to live satisfactorily in the dialectic of freedom and responsibility. The Christian therapist believes that this can be accomplished in Christ. Paul Tournier puts it well in his The Meaning of Persons (1957):

> We are not called upon to impose our own scale of values on our patients. But if we help them to recover the fundamental function of life, namely choice, sooner or later they will raise the question of values--the dialogue will become spiritual. I cannot at this point break off the dialogue on the grounds that I am neither a philosopher nor theologian, but merely a doctor. What I must do then is to know what my own convictions are and take responsibility for them, without attempting to impose them on others. (p.215)

208

It seems to me that at a certain point in the
therapeutic program it becomes not only an opportunity but also an obligation to present value options to
the patient. In any case, it will be done with one's
eyes open, or blindly, either as a fundamental to the
therapeutic goals or inexorably out of the sheer fact
that the therapist is also a human being. Christian
therapy, as I view it, entails an exposition rather
than an imposition of values.

I, as a Christian therapist, attempt to affect
a compromise between the extremes of non-directive
counseling, in which the counselor endeavors to portray an amoral, objective, impersonal person, and the
fallacy of authoritative directiveness, which tends to
usurp both the freedom and the responsibility of the
patient. It is an attempt to interact in a living
dialogue; a mutual enterprise for the achievement of
emotional well-being and personal growth.

This approach tends to be set in the context of
the ideas of counseling for the Christian psychologist. Although these ideals are not always attained
for me, nonetheless, this is the goal to which I give
myself. At the presumed mid-point of my vocational
career, I find it both inciting and exciting.

IX.

FAITH IN ACADEMICS AND RESEARCH

Many psychologists function as members of the faculty in educational institutions of higher learning. Their positions in teaching, research and administration are not often thought to be directly related to their religious faith. Yet it is the conviction of the writers in this section that what they do in these roles is directly related to their Christianity.

Dr. Dittes is an administrator and academic advisor. He directs educational programs in a major university. He perceives his role as one of assisting persons in reaching their goals. He attempts to humanize procedures and to make programs serve people. He is convinced that Christian values and a desire to minister guides his endeavors.

Dr. Gorsuch is a meticulous researcher. He often thought of becoming a parish minister but decided to engage in basic research and theorizing which would serve the church. He writes of much work with churches and denominations on such basic concerns as training children in moral values. As He says, "I am a minister to ministers".

Dr. Strunk is deeply involved in the education of ministers and the training of pastoral counselors. He teaches and directs research at the same time that he supervises and counsels. As any one who is a part of professional education will recognize, the role of professor in these progrsms is multifaceted. He sees his faith as the foundation for whatever he does.

These psychologists illustrate yet another way that psychology and faith can be related.

James E. Dittes is a psychologist who also is
seminary trained. He has spent his entire career on
the faculties of Yale University, where he is now
chairman of the Department of Religious Studies, as
well as a faculty member of the Divinity School and
of the Department of Psychology. He has written
The Church in the Way, Minister on the Spot,
Bias and the Pious, and the forthcoming Ministry:
Called in Question. In addition to having edited the
Journal for the Scientific Study of Religion, he
also has been president of the Society for the
Scientific Study of Religion.

An Enabling Ministry in Academics and Administration
by
James E. Dittes

If people are surprised when one calls oneself
both "Psychologist" and Christian", it is usually
because they perceive a conflict between the two. If
they think the conflict has been resolved, people
surmise it is at the expense of a compromise. Yet I
do not view myself as caught in a role conflict. Nor
do I see myself as less a Christian or any less a
Psychologist because I profess to be a psychologist
who is a Christian.

Instead of a conflict I would say confluence. I
feel the two reinforce each other. I would add a
hyphen between 'psychologist' and 'Christian' to
avoid the impression that one limits or constricts
the other.

On Outlook not a Role

Furthermore, I do not think of being a Christian
or being a psychologist as roles I play. Four roles I
play are as teacher, researcher, administrator and
counselor. Being a psychologist and being a Christian
are characteristics of outlooks I bring to these
roles, I would like to think I am different and more
adequate in all these roles because I am a psychologist-Christian.

Let me detail some of my duties. Then I shall
comment on the difference my being a psychologist-
Christian makes.

I teach classes in the psychology of religion,
pastoral theology and religious research. For a number
of years I edited the Journal for the Scientific Study
of Religion. For sometime, I was the director of the
doctoral program in religious studies at Yale University and more recently chairman of the Department of
Religious Studies. I have been a part of major research on ministerial leadership. I regularly am a
part of boards and cmmittees which set policy for
church bodies as well as the University. I continue
to offer much personal counseling to students on both
academic and personal matters. However, in all these
endeavors I consider myself essentially a "teacher".

Essentially a "Teacher"

Why do I say all of these activities are clearly "teaching"? Teaching to me is the art of making the implicit explicit and of making the latent manifest. It is the task of mobilizing others' resources of insight and of action, and of evoking from others a clearer sense of their perception of the world and of their destiny in it. It is like the sculptor chipping away the waste from the stone until the form it imbedded all the time is visible. It is like the artist putting onto canbas, or onto a stage, patterns that provide others with expression and recognition.

As an editor, for example, my principal job was to help each author get his or her point across. I think it is necessary as an editor to immerse oneself into the thinking of the author, just as thoroughly as a counselor gets inside the struggles of a counselee, or a teacher the searchings of a student. The question here is: Just what is the significance of the author's contribution, and how can that significance be made most clear? I seldom "rejected" a manuscript outright, even though the Journal had space for only a fraction of the manuscripts that were submitted. I even less often, almost never, "accepted" a manuscript. My usual response was to suggest to the author the way that I thought his or her points could be established to a degree that would warrant and receive serious attention from readers. I wanted the author's real contribution to emerge clearly. Sometimes this meant encouraging rewriting and rearrangement of materials. Sometimes it meant inviting the author to help the editor invent novel typographical formats to accommodate the particular material. Sometimes it meant encouraging an author to be more adventurour and less pedantic in giving the manuscript a title that would communicate.

While some writers objected to my editing, most seemed delighted to be encouraged and accompanied in the creative task of getting their ideas and their research across. That is also my experience when I adopt the same style in other roles. I see myself as working best when I am a facilitator, clarifier, mobilizer and companion.

Does this approach sound like that of a psychological counselor? Or a pastor? Does it sound like the role any Christian would assume? I hope so, because this is the psychologist-Christian style in which I have tried to fashion my vocation.

Perhaps the most important characteristic of the style of my vocation that I aspire to is the ability to immerse oneself, with the utmost of one's faculty for perception and reflection, in the thoughts and experiences of others, be they students, committee members or research subjects. This requires something like recklessly abandoning one's own identity while, at the same time, fiercely retaining, with keyed-up sharpness, those qualities of ego-functioning that permit one to transcend and reflect on the experience. And I know that the degree to which I can achieve such a style is directly a result of having been endowed with such traits from my experience as a psychologist and from my experience as a Christian.

I repeat my testimony that I find my experience as a psychologist and my experience as a Christian reinforcing each other, not challenging or contradicting each other. Let me now try to describe some of these traits that enable one to fill my vocational roles with the style of self-abandonment and immersion, and let me testify as to how I see each of these traits developing out of my experience as a psychologist and my experience as a Christian.

Prime Convictions

There is, first of all, simply put, the conviction that others are worth it, that their goals are worth pursuing, that their insights are worth attending to and developing. Such a conviction comes more easily, I think, to one who has been exposed as a psychologist to the richness and diversity and resourcefulness of the human personality, and exposed as a Christian to an awareness of the goodness of God's creation and the power and availability of His recreative presence.

But doesn't the psychologist know too much of illness and the Christian too much of sin? The other person may be leading in widely distorting and destructive directions that need correction, not encouragement. The psychologist-Christian can comprehend this disruption in proper perspective. He or she has that freedom to face it because of being able to take it

214

more seriously than one who is neither a psychologist nor a Christian or one who is only a psychologist or a Christian.

The symptoms of illness/sin don't just happen. They are not surprising, fearful demons. These distortions are a natural and expected part of human nature--whether we expect them as psychologists or as Christians. They arise inexorably and intelligibly out of circumstances and encounters. They have a concreteness and a meaning. The psychologist and the Christian attend to these disruptions earnestly for the meaning they do convey and does not shrink in anger or threat because they are disruptions.

Because the psychologist-Christian knows that these disruptions are transcended by being part of an ongoing larger context of human experience, the intimidation and dislike they might otherwise produce are transcended. An illogical shift in the presentation at a committee meeting or in class, a persistent inappropriate recital of unnecessary and irrelevant details in a manuscript or in a counseling session, failure of a research subject to complete certain questionnaire items--such things are not merely annoyances to be scolded or wished away. They become further data, further interpretable clues that something important is happening. I have ventured, in one whole book, The Church in the Way (1967), to show the understanding and constructive use of such thwarting can be an important tool for the Christian pastor.

Knowledge About Myself

More profoundly, however, than what experience as a Christian and as a psychologist enables one to understand about others is what this experience enables one to understand about oneself. It frees one from the stalwart self-directedness that American individualism has so generously admired. Psychologist-Christians can feel already justified and do not need to set up their own good works. They have resources that help them to be free from the need to ensure their own sense of selfhood and of validity by imposing control and agenda in their professional encounters. With less of a feeling of having already been justified, one might impose more vigorously one's own definitions of problems and solutions on one's students and counselees. As an editor, one might have to cling

215

more to canons of scientific methodology and scholarly writing style and require authors to accommodate to
one's criteria, rather than to put oneself at the service of the authors. As an academic administrator or
as a chairman of a committee, one might find oneself
standing more firmly against creative proposals.

Psychologists are fortunate in being able to have
learned to garner some sense of identity and compent-
ence precisely from the act of attending to others.
They are "doing their own thing" precisely when they
are most immersed in the affairs of others. In a way
that the Scripture does not mean, they are finding
themselves when they are losing themselves in the
experiences and insights of others. But if their
identities as psychologists are fostered by losing
their personal identity and self-directiveness in
these limited ways, so are their identities as Christians similarly fostered by losing themselves in the
affairs of others. In different, yet complementing
ways, both psychologists and Christians are doing
their own thing when they are most involved with
others.

What Needs Doing . . . Has been Done

But, beyond this, experience as Christians frees
persons from needing to do their own thing, even their
own thing as Christians. What most needs doing has
already been done for them. So they can sit looser
to all temptations to impose themselves as teachers
or editors or administrators or researchers or
counselors on others—since they do not need to be
"good" teachers or editors or administrators or researchers or counselors by any conventional marks of
these roles. They can offer themselves in these roles
to others.

Free and other—directed though they may be,
psychologist-Christians are not irresponsibly undi-
rected or non-directed. Their experience as Christians and as psychologists make them know tow things
too keenly to be without a strong sense of stewardship and responsibility. As psychologists and as
Christians they know what has been done for them;
they also know that their own response to a situation
does count and does make a difference. They dare not

216

be whimsical and casual about where and how they invest their energies and time, or about how they guide others. So much has been invested in them that they must be prudent as to how they invest themselves and invite others to invest themselves. Their "other-directedness" then follows as the most responsible way they can give expression to such earnest concerns. They invest themselves all the more and all the more carefully and attentively because of this sense of responsibility and stewardship that derives jointly from being Christians and being psychologists.

Herein Lies Risk

There is, indeed, risk, almost deadly risk, in the professional style I have been describing--and this is the heart of my testimony. It is the risk I have described as "something like recklessly abandoning one's own identity" while immersing oneself in the struggling, often inchoate perceptions of others. As a professor, I am supposed to know something, to have perspective and information and skills of analysis which I have mastered and which I am prepared to transmit to others. Without this, I can hardly lay claim to being a professor. Is it not lost when I teach essentially inductively, via case studies and discussion? Similarly, as an editor, I can be expected to have a commanding view of the field, to know which frontiers can be fruitfully worked at and which are presently impenetrable and why; and I might be expected to use this broad insight in soliciting selecting, and shaping articles. Similarly, as an administrator, should I not have a vision of goals and principles, a sense of tradition and heritage which should guide and shape the planning of a student for his or her studies and of a committee for a curriculum? To immerse myself into the partialness and particularity of any single case study or research project or classroom discussion or the opinions and searchings of a single student--is not this style I have described the abdication of my necessary role, the repudiation of others' expectations of me, and the loss of my own professional authority and identity? There are those who would--and do--say so.

But my experience as a psychologist and my experience as a Christian both lead me to conclude that

properly "authoritative" and conventional and safe
such ways of exercising--almost flaunting--my professional role are unnecessary, false and illusory.
My experience as a psychologist-Christian convinces
me that heritage, principles, destiny, wisdom, revelation, vocation--all these matters that the professional knows so well in abstraction--do not significantly exist except as they are encountered precisely
in the partialness and particularity of personal relationships. I fall short of my responsibility as
professor, editor, administrator, counselor, until I
can help others to discern in their own concrete
experience, inchoate and incomplete as it may be,
those perspectives and principles which I profess to
be attuned to.

Encountering God In Historical Events

     As a Christian, I have learned that God's ways
are not best discerned to regulations sent down from
a mountain top to be codified and transmitted by ex-
perts--as the Hebrews sometimes supposed. Nor are they
best understood in abstract ideas or ideals, as the
Greeks often thought. Nor are they best found in
studied attempts to more beyond consciousness, as
Eastern religions often suggest. Rather, the Christian has encountered God in such unlikely places as the
history of a small, wandering, frequently exiled
tribe, in the story of a Baby in a manger, in the life
and mean death of a carpenter-turned-wandering-teacher
and in the personal and political struggles of a
people and of an institution who dare call themselves
"the body of Christ".

     As a spychologist-Christian I have become con-
vinced that that which transcends any human experience, to judge and guide and save it, can judge,
guide, and save only as it enters into particular
human experience. In any "incarnation", the trans-
cendent always risks being distorted and enjulfed by
the particularities and by their chaos and conflict.
This is the risk the professor or editor or counselor
or administrator takes when he or she invests himself
or herself. But it is a risk we are enabled to take
because, on our behalf, it is the risk that God has
taken, in His act of creation and in His act of
salvation.

218

Richard L. Gorsuch is a social psychologist, research methodologist, and ordained Disciples of Christ Minister. He is the editor of the _Journal for the Scientific Study of Religion_, one of the most respected publications in the field. He has published books on _Factor Analysis_ and The _Nature of Man: A Social Psychological Perspective_, the latter of which shows his primary interests. He has consulted widely with churches and denominations. At the time of this writing he was at George Peabody College. At present he is Professor of Social Work and Psychology at the University of Texas at Arlington, Arlington, Texas.

Research Psychology:
An Indirect Ministry to the Ministry

by
Richard L. Gorsuch

Psychology was not my original vocational goal,
but only became my occupational preference several
years after I obtained·a Doctor of Philosophy degree
in Psychology. My original occupational goal was the
pastoral ministry. Being a minister would, I thought,
best bring meaning to my life by serving God and people
while also using the capabilities I had. To achieve
this goal required appropriate studies, and so I entered Texas Christian University to obtain a Bachelor's
degree as a prerequisite to seminary training.

In casting for an appropriate undergraduate major,
I decided to choose one that would aid me in my service
as a minister. Making the usual assumptions that those
not intimately connected with the field make. I decided to major in psychology. My purpose was not to
study psychology as a discipline, but to learn more
of the nature of contemporary people. Such knowledge
would, I presumed, enable me to enter more effectively
into the lives of those whom I would be servinc.

College Study in Psychology: A hope

Those of you who know psychology will not be surprised to hear that I did not find a great deal in psychology that was directly relevant to the usual activities of a minister. But I took hope because psychology
was pursuing one of the most valuable topics ever
studied--people. I hoped that such study would provide
invaluable information about the way God has formed us.
I had confidence that such knowledge would be just as
useful as the knowledge of the empirical world which
enables us to be free of the task of personally growing
our own food. Because of that hope, and the thought
that deeper psychology might contain the information I
yet lacked, I decided to accept the opportunity to study
for a Ph.D. in psychology at the University of Illinois.
"Accept the opportunity" is the best description, since
I did not work hard for it. Rather, my psychology

professors encouraged me to go on. Dr. Saul Sells was
particularly helpful, not only in his interest and encouragement, but also in placing me as a research
assistant to Dr. Raymond B. Cattell at Illinois.

I was willing to pursue a graduate degree in
psychology before studying theology in part because of
my solid interest in the ministry. While I knew that
I would study for a graduate degree in theology regardless of my psychological studies, I could not be sure
that the reverse would be true. Not only might the
gates to psychology have been less open after a sojourn in the foreign land of theology, but I might not
have been able to resist the temptation to move into a
real life setting.

Psychology and Values

Graduate school in psychology was an interesting
experience. It quickly became apparent that not even
the top psychologists of 1960 really knew much more
then the theologians about how people became committed
to the beliefs and values they serve. And yet those
beliefs and values, including the religious ones, often
dominate a person's life so much that they dictate not
only how that person lives but also how he/she dies.

The sketchiness of research on beliefs and values
did not seem to be a function of its being inappropriate to psychology. Indeed, it was a topic of vital
interest to those early psychologists who have contrib-
ted the most to modern psychology. William James, for
example, discussed the nature of the spiritual man in
his introductory psychology text Psychology: The
Briefer Course (James, 1892). Even Wundt, the founder
of the experimental branch of psychology, considered
the topic of sufficient importance to devote three
volumes to it. This series was entitled Ethics: An
Investigation of the Facts and Laws of the Moral Life
(Wundt, 1903). C. Stanley Hall, another founding
father of American psychology, was a prominent figure
in the investigation of religious phenomena, and felt
that love and altruism were the true ends of life.
Certainly the early figures thought the study of
values--which includes the study of ethics, morality
and religion--was a vital and necessary part of a complete study of man.

It appeared to me that the lack of research on values had been a function of several influences. First is the complexity of the phenomena. Persons are difficult to understand. How they become committed to their values is not as easy to investigate as, for example, reinforcement schedules. It is only by the aid of both modern computing devices and the information provided by studies of the simpler areas of psychology that progress can be made in the understanding of values.

Another factor in the hiatus on research into values came from the results from early studies. Some of their findings were not particularly encouraging. For example, the extensive set of studies by Hartshorne and May (e.g., 1927) produced the conclusion that there is no such thing as an honest or dishonest child. Most children's cheating depended more on the pressures and opportunities than, for example, how much they valued honest behavior. The effect of church and Sunday School was found to be trivial to non-existent. (Actually, Hartshorne and May's work is less discouraging--but still challenging--from a theological perspective. It can be interpreted as showing that the statement that all men are sinners applies to children as well as to adults, and that the church is the coming together of sinners rather than gathered saints. In addition, a theological perspective is more concerned with what man can be, rather than with what man is, and it has generally been skeptical about the church's ability to create the ideal man).

In addition, the research on value commitment seemed to have diminished because of the temper of the times. The general intellectual environment of psychology was not supportive of work in this area during and after World War II. Instead, religion and values were generally seen as topics of interest to only the lunatic fringe. This feeling still seems to exist in the more traditionally academically oriented psychology departments, but, fortunately, the climate is changing. Not only was I encouraged in my interest by professors such as Cattell, but the 1960's saw a revival of interest in basic issues of value commitment. Psychologists such as Aronfreed, Bronfenbrenner, Hoffman, Kohlberg, Rosenhan, Rokeach, and Scott, in addition to others, have all contributed to the area. Much of this is summarized elsewhere (cf. Gorsuch, 1973).

222

Since graduate studies in psychology did not include much about value commitment per se, I found myself devoting a considerable amount of my graduate school time to methodological issues. At least I could learn how to identify, measure and statistically analyze psychological phenomena, I thought.

Ministry as a Problem, Psychology as a Solution

After my years in residence at the University of Illinois, I entered Vanderbilt Divinity School to study for my Bachelor of Divinity degree. Here, too, how man becomes committed to values was not discussed. Unfortunately, the topic did not appear even to be of interest to many of the faculty and students. Their concerns were more with the traditional questions of theology and personal faith.

At the end of my career as a student, I had to decide between the pastorate and psychology. But I still had little notion of how I could help people develop and clarify their beliefs and values. Neither the study of psychology nor the professional ministry left me with any confidence that I could pastor a flock in this vital task. I knew I could do what everyone else was doing, but studies such as those of Hartshorne and May did not convince me that the professional ministry really did more than comfort people. This is not to disparage the role of pastor as comforter, for that is a most vital one; it is only to say that if I were going to be a minister, I wanted to be an agent of growth as well.

So I decided to become a research-oriented psychologist. As such, I would have an opportunity to investigate the phenomena that I felt were the most meaningful: the role of beliefs and values in man's life and how persons become committed to those values. I would provide an indirect ministery to ministers, so that those who come later would be better able to carry out their ministry.

Implications of being a Theologically Oriented Psychologist

The decision to investigate values as a psychologist carried with it a commitment to the total area of psychology as well. This was for several reasons.

223

First, it is only being concerned with the basic
issues being investigated in psychology that one can
capitalize upon them to benefit his own area of research. Then, too, research-oriented positions are
seldom available which are purely research in an area
such as values. Instead, one usually works in an
academic department and thus has a responsibility for
teaching. This teaching invariably involves much
broader areas than just values. And if the psychology
departments looking for personnel were totally unin-
terested in a values-oriented psychologist, I was prepared to teach psychology and pursue some non-value
oriented research as a form of "tent-making" to support my own research interest. I will also have to
admit that most topics which psychologists find interesting are fascinating to me as well, thus supporting
a general commitment to the discipline.

The method of my entry into psychology has provided a certain degree of objectivity towards the area.
My commitments are less to psychology as a discipline
that to the development of the long range benefits
that might accrue from psychological research. Being
convinced of the validity of Kurt Lewin's (the famous
social psychologist) statement that "the most practical
thing is a good theory", I am firmly supportive of
basic research. But it is of much lesser importance
whether the discipline receiving credit for a major
insight be psychology, biology, sociology, social work,
or theology. I picked psychology because I feel it is
the best for long range benefits towards my knowledge-
oriented goals. I still feel a little odd about being
labeled a "psychologist".

My feeling of objectivity towards the discipline
also comes from my theology training. During my
seminary days, I was able to view psychology from the
outside. It also provided the skills of another profession by which I could make a contribution to society,
if psychology would turn out to be a major disappointment. Having another profession to fall back on con-
tributes marvelously towards an objective approach to
one's current profession!

Being a psychologist has not been without its
theological problems. I originally became committed to
the Christian faith through a search for meaning in
life. I found that meaning within the faith and within the idea of serving through the ministry. But my
current work may be sufficient to give meaning to life
in and by itself. There is nothing in the work I do
that requires the Christian faith as a necessary
224

prerequisite or life within the Church to support it. This lessens my own personal need for Christianity although not my basic convictions.

Life within the institutional church has been made more difficult by my knowledge of psychological research. This research has found it easier to document religion's faults than its achievements. It has been difficult to show that religious people are much different from non-religious people outside of the specifically religious behaviors such as going to church. This applies regardless of how "religious" is defined. Indeed, one of the few areas of morality where religious people are obviously different from non-religious is that of sex. Religious people are less promiscuous than non-religious people. Numerous studies ranging from Kinsey's reports to our present data on college student values have found this to be true. This little investigated phenomena is at least well hallowed by time. Both the Old and New Testament show a definite concern with sexual mores. But why haven't we been able to show Christians are also distinctive in the other concerns hallowed by time, such as love of neighbor?

A more subtle problem comes from the intersection of my theology and my work. My work derives from my theology, and so it is easy to build a super-justification of the work which can become idolatrous in its own right. Since my research is an extension of the work of the church, what difference does it make if I participate in the institutional church? Given what does not happen in most churches, my research could be more important than the contribution I could make to a congregation. But this is, of course, basically the same kind of temptation that encourages a minister to neglect his own family for the sake of the institution.

Extending the Psychology of Values

Due to good luck or the grace of God--depending on your theology--the position which I obtained upon completing theology school in 1968 was specifically concerned with how people become committed to values, a Kennedy chair established with the John F. Kennedy Center for Research on Education and Human Development at George Peabody College for Teachers. A Professorship is defined with a reasonable amount of

225

freedom. The problems that I investigate are those
which I choose to investigate, with the understanding
that most of them will be related to my basic appointment. As a member of the Peabody faculty I do a
limited amount of teaching and direct the research of
some students. Since the work is mostly with graduate students, I am able to treat problems in greater
depth than would otherwise be possible.

In a typical year, I might teach the following
courses:

Psychology 261: Ethical and Moral Development
    This course examines research on the trends in
    ethics and moral behavior of children and youth.
    Cognitive and learning theory approaches are
    discussed as well as the role of the family,
    peers, church, and school.

Psychology 313: Factor Analysis
    This course is designed to develop understand-
    ing of the factor analytic model and the most
    frequently applied computational methods.
    (Psychology 313 is my contribution to the general
    graduate program and grows out of my past empha-
    sis on methodology.)

Psychology 369: Advanced Seminar in Developmental
    Psychology
    Cognitive State Theories of Moral Development
    In this seminar we examine stage theories of
    Kohlberg, Piaget, and others concerned with
    ethical development. The seminar format allows
    us considerable flexibility in examining the
    topic.

Psychology 262w: Value Development in Children and
    Youth
    This is a summer workshop offered jointly with
    the education department. In it we attempt to
    train those who work directly with children. The
    training is focused on how adult workers can help
    each child clarify his own values and confront
    ethical problems in a more mature fashion.
    Indoctrination is, of course, discouraged.

Unlike many psychology departments, the Peabody
faculty is sympathetic towards research on values. They
are deeply concerned with the impact of psychology on
the quality of human life and with social issues as
well.   226

Fortunately, their concerns are not of the "bleeding heart" variety. Rather, they are strictly oriented towards knowledge substantiated by hard data and towards theories that can be checked against empirical data. After joining the faculty, I heard that some members had been skeptical of the position in moral and ethical development. They were afraid that it might be filled with some strange creature. My methodological background was reassuring to them; it was reassuring to me to know that even the more skittish were interested in having the position filled.

Besides teaching, my work is concerned with research in the area of value commitment itself. At present, this research is typically observational in nature. We learn by talking with people and analyzing their responses as a function of other variables. To save time, we often use a questionnaire format to gather people's ideas. Note that we do not necessarily take their comments at face value but integrate them with other information as necessary to solve the problem at hand.

Current Research

In any given year I am involved in several research projects. For example, the major ones of 1970, when this paper was originally written, were:

Value Conflicts in the School Setting: The schools are relatively homogeneious in terms of the values which they espouse. But students enter the public schools from a wide range of backgrounds and are diverse in the values which they hold. The value conflicts thus generated will probably be manifested by the child being a behavioral problem to others or by the child having personality problems and being anxious, as well as by lowered achievement. This project measured value conflicts in the school setting of children from various backgrounds and determined the impact of those conflicts.

Note that this project is of mutual interest to those of us interested in basic value commitment and to the public school system as well. Only as we understand the range of value differences and how they affect interpersonal behavior can we help reconcile man to man--or, in this case, teacher to pupil. Because of its interest to education, the United States Office of Education gave us a two year grant to pursue the topic. 227

We collected data from children in sixteen different classrooms on their values (children only participate with the permission of their parents who have, fortunately, been generally willing). The teachers rated their children on the various values which each child actually shows as well as reporting all important incidents occurring during the semester. We examine these data for such factors as the effects of the peer group and of the teacher on changes in a child's values over the semester; both of these were strong but the teacher's effects were strongest. We also found that most problems in the classroom are a function of values conflicts.

Changes in the Ethical Judgments of College Students Over the Past Forty Years: In 1929, 1939, 1949, and 1958 a scale requiring ethical judgments of various behaviors was given to college students in Illinois, Ohio, and Wyoming. Our project involved returning to those same colleges in 1969 and comparing the results to those of the earlier studies. The general trends suggest little overall change in values (Gorsuch and Daly, 1970). The basic considerations on which a society is built have remained equally valued across the years. The only major changes involved an increased leniency of attitude towards premarital sex and less concern with religious values. But even here the differences within the present generation of college students are nevertheless much greater than those between the generations. The "generation gap" does not appear to be in basic values, other than those of sex and religion, as measured by this scale. This project has been supported out of a general grant to the Kennedy Center by Biomedical Sciences Support Grant FR-07087-04 from the General Research Support Branch, Division of Research Resources, Bureau of Health Professions Education and Manpower Training, National Institutes of health.

Developing and Efficient Instrument for Determining Stages of Moral Development: Kohlberg (1968) found in his research that children at different ages approach ethical questions in different ways. The young child, for example, will evaluate moral questions in terms of his own subjective benefit. As he grows older, he begins to take other people's feelings into account. At. At the highest stages, reached by only a minority of adults, moral and ethical decisions are

228

based on basic ethical principles. How a person moves from the earlier stages to the later ones is a question of vital importance.

Unfortunately, it is sometimes difficult to study this movement because it is hard to evaluate what stage a child is at. This project was designed to find more efficient ways to determine the stage of development as a step towards more research on the stages themselves, and has involved John O'Conner and Farzad Shamsavari. It has also been supported by a Biomedical Sciences Support Grant, Bureau of Health Professions Education and Manpower Training, National Institutes of Health. The result has been the Defining Issues Scale with, with some changes, has been used in an extensive program of research by James Rest and his associates.

Critical Appraisal of Research on Socialization: Saul Sells, under the sponsorhsip of the United States Offices of Education, organized a review of the affective areas of psychology. The task was to identify the major points where further research is needed. The affective domain was divided into a series of sur-areas, each of which is to produce a report. I gathered together several of the major investigators in the area of socialization to report on that field.

Socialization is a broader domain than just value commitment since it includes all of the aspects of how the child becomes a member of human society. But it certainly includes value commitment. Indeed, some of our research suggests that the two are essentially the same in the child. One must learn those values which allow him/her to become an effective member of groups before she/he can become committed to what are generally known as the higher values.

It should be obvious from the size of these projects that I do not do them alone. Other psychologists, such as Robert Newbrough on the value conflict project, were co-investigators with me. In addition, graduate students are employed on the projects. Without the dedicated help of these fellow psychologists--both pre and post Ph.D.--and of the secretaries, progress would be very slow indeed.

229

My Graduate Student's Research

In my role as advisor to graduate students, I
have the privilege of participating indirectly with
a variety of research projects. In the present graduate school system, students generally select professors who are in an area of joint interest, and the
project proceeds from that interest. The student is
the final authority on how the project is to be conceptualized, but I naturally enter into the process.
Here are some samples of what graduate students working with me during 1970 were investigating:

Effects of Parents' Childrearing Practices on
Their Child's Ethical Development:

It is generally assumed that parents are the major
source of a child's values. Paul Shoffeitt examined the
way parents work with their children. He related this
to both the stage and content of the child's ethical
development. He has several hypotheses which have developed out of the past research. For example, he
expects that those parents who discuss moral issues
at a level only slightly above that of their child
will have a more beneficial effect than those who
either talk at the same level at which the child thinks
or those who talk over their child's head. He also expects that some childrearing practices will be effective only if there is a positive relationship between
the parents and the child.

Religion and Prejudice: As noted earlier, there
is a consistent relationship between religion and prejudice with the more religious being generally more
prejudiced. Daniel Alshire is interested in identifying more exactly this relationship. For example, some
have suggested that it is only the moderately religious
that are more prejudiced, while those deeply involved
in the life of the church are among the least prejudiced. Further, some theorize that there are two different types of religious people; those involved in the
faith for what they can get out of it are the more
prejudiced, while those who are committed to the faith
for the sake of the faith are less prejudiced than
many others. A further question is the interesting one
of whether or not serious study of the Christian
doctrines of brotherhood will change scores on measures of prejudice. This study was conducted by an extensive review of the literature.

230

Consultation

My background in research methodology and theology has also led to consultative involvements. For
example, I occasionally review manuscripts submitted to
journals to aid the editor in deciding whether or not
it will make a worthwhile contribution. But my major
source of other involvements takes the form of consulting with new or ongoing projects. I am called in
on research projects being undertaken by various denominational agencies to help them think through their
problems and possibilities.

Another area of consultation is with research being
done by colleagues whose projects border on my area. For
example, I and William Wallace worked with Gilbert
James' study of seminarian ghetto experiences. During
the summer months James took a group of students to the
Chicago ghetto so that they can encounter the poverty
life as it actually is. William Wallace and I aided
in the evaluation of the effect of these experiences.
Preliminary data suggested, for example, that the
students show little change in their basically religious feelings but do change some of their ideas. Such
consultation allows me to share my training with those
expertise is in other compatible areas. Few of my projects are directly concerned with what a minister
might do to aid the belief and value development of
his congregation. But they form the necessary background out of which such projects develop. For it is
only as we come to understand how people become committed to beliefs and values that any person--parent
or pastor--can use that knowledge to build programs
and develop relationships that will change people's
lives. In that sense I continue to view my research
as an indirect ministry to the ministry of the church.

REFERENCES

Gorsuch, R. L. Educating from a contemporary theory
of man as an ethical being. Educational Forum,
1977, 37, 1969-1978.

Gorsuch, R. L. and Daly, W. Changes in ethical
judgments of college students: 1958-1969.
Proceedings, 78th Annual Convention. The
American Psychological Association, 1970.

Hartshorne, H., May, M. A., et al. Testing the knowledge of right and wrong.
Religious Education Association Monograph #1,
1927.

James, W. Psychology. New York: Harper and Brothers,
1961 (original 1892).

Kohlberg, L. The child as a moral philosopher.
Psychology Today, 1968, pp. 25-30.

Wundt, W. Ethics: An investigation of the facts and
laws of the moral life. Vol. I: Introduction and
the facts of the moral life; Vol. II: Ethical
systems; Vol. III: The principles of morality and
the departments of the moral life. New York:
McMillan, 1903.

Orlo Strunk, Jr. is Professor of the Psychology of Religion at Boston University. He is one of the foremost figures in the current resurgence of interest in the psychology of religion. He has edited such books as Readings in the Psychology of Religion and The Psychology of Religion: Historic and Interpretative Readings. He has authored Religion: A Psychological Interpretation, The Choice Called Atheism and The Secret Self. He is president-elect of the American Psychological Association; Division 36, Psychologist Interested in Religious Issues.

All things Hold Together
by
Orlo Strunk, Jr.

Life--A Mystery

After spending five years in the world of business
I turned to the liberal arts, to the study of Biblical
literature and philosophy, and later, at age twenty-six
to the Christian ministry. Two convictions have become increasingly clear to me as I have occupied these
years since that time in academic and religious endeavor. First, I am convinced life is more a mystery
to be lived than a problem to be solved. Next, I am
convinced that life is more important than profession.

With these introductory remarks I do not wish to
suggest that this insight came upon me in some mysterious way, or was a by-product of some exotic exercise
or the stirrings of a psychadelic trip. Nothing that
dramatic at all! In fact, the genesis of such a
simple conclusion had come to me in many forms (and at
various times) long before my fortieth birthday.

These convictions first took on sharp awareness
about ten years ago while interviewing a candidate for
a teaching position in a small liberal arts college
where I was serving as academic dean. The applicant
was a professor of history in a prestigious mid-
western university. Some of the committee members
could not quite understand why he would wish to re-
linquish his tenured position to join our relatively
isolated college faculty. He explained:

Frankly, life seems to me far more important
than my professional advancement. At the
university I am under continuous pressure to
publish, to achieve amid professional competition, and to commit myself to all kinds
of strains. I would much rather be a good
teacher in a community which values personal relationships between teacher and student.

This was not an easy decision for him, nor was it
a simple one without conflict and dynamic. But I suspect that in one form or another such a thesis presents itself to most professional persons.

234

Nearly thirty years ago a psychologist suggested the possibility of three "character-types"
--the Seinsmensch, the Lebensmensch, and the Leistung-
smench. The Seinsmensch is the person who goes on
living, showing no particular goal in life. The
Lebensmensch is somewhat easygoing in lifestyle, hop-
ing to taste a wide range of life's many offerings.
The Leistungsmensch is the striving type, one de-
sirous to achieve. Undoubtedly, these last two types
are present in most professional people. I sense both
of them moving in my own life and at different times
one seems to dominate. Here I am saying that in recent years, the Lebensmensch has taken on an abundance
of meaning for me. It tends to guide me in regard to
choices having to do with my professional activities.

These two very general themes--that life is a
mystery to be lived rather than a problem to be solved
and that a full life is more important than a professional project seem to me to be necessary introductory comments if my treatment of the faith-profession
relationship is to appear real and human.

But what, given all this, do I do as a psychologist, professor, counselor, administrator and writer?
How do these various activities take form in the faith-
profession relationship?

A Typical Day

The beginning of an answer may be seen in terms
of a report of a "typical" day. I'll pick a Tuesday
because that day of the week usually finds me touching
all facets of my work. In the hope of continuing the
personal orientation of this chapter, I'll describe an
honest-to-goodness report with as many details as
brevity will permit:

8:00-9:00. Commuting. I live about twenty-six
miles south-east of Boston and it takes me about an
hour to make the trip to the University. Although commuting time is often counted as "wasted" by many, for
me this is not at all true. Another member of my
academic department commutes with me. We are this
morning hour to talk about all kinds of matters, both
personal and professional. Together our commuting
conversations cover a wide range of theoretical and
practical interests. There is a sense in which this
is a "commuting seminar," integral to my professional and academic life.   235

9:00-10:00. Counseling. Ordinarily, I schedule this hour for continuous counseling or supervision in the Albert V. Danielsen Pastoral Counseling Center of Boston University School of Theology. On this particular day I am seeing a client for the seventeenth time.

10:00-10:45. Worship. I try to attend the school's regular worship service at this time. I have discovered that I need some kind of regular devotional discipline, either private or communal.

10:45-11:10. Class Preparation. This brief period is used to review class notes or to check on library references.

11:10-12:30. Class. During this period I teach a class in the psychology of religion. Since this particular class is an elective for first professional degree candidates, it usually attracts about thirty students with a wide range of exposure to psychological science.

12:30-1:10. Lunch. Besides using this forty-minute period for eating, I frequently employ it to chat with out graduate assistant or with a doctoral candidate about dissertation plans.

1:10-2:00 Counseling intake. I attempt to keep this slot free for talking with new clients at the Danielsen Center, in which I serve as a faculty counselor.

2:10-3:00 Counseling. Usually this spot is used for continuous counseling. On this particular day, I am seeing a client for the twenty-first time.

3:00-4:00. Library work. During this hour I check out references and bibliographical items in regard to my writing. I do all my writing at home on weekends, and in the summer.

4:00-5:30. Staff Meeting. This weekly meeting brings together the eight doctoral candidates who are serving as counseling fellows in the Albert V. Danielsen Pastoral Counseling Center. The meeting is chaired by the Center's Director of Training. A consulting psychiatrist is always in attendance. It is essentially a diagnostic type conference, in which many issues of pastoral counseling are discussed.

5:30-6:00. Dinner. Usually I eat with several of the doctoral candidates serving as pastoral counseling fellows.

6:10-7:30. Research. I try to use this period to attend to research activities--sometimes library research, at other times statistical.

7:30-8:30. Administration. As Chairman of the Area of Religion and the Social Sciences and a member of three faculty committees, there are always administrative details waiting to be handled.

Of course, this Tuesday outline is typical only in the sense that it touches most of my expressions of ministry--teaching, counseling, administering and research-writing. In actual practice, days vary greatly. On Mondays, for example, I take my "professional day" and use it to prepare lectures, write and edit book reviews, and read. Wednesdays are almost always filled with committee meetings and library research, with no counseling and no classroom work.

Related interests

These, then, are the professional things I do within the faith-profession relationship. Naturally, out of them evolve special interests which tend to color my everyday responsibilities. My long-standing interest in attempting to get a firm psychological understanding of religion makes the psychology of religion my major academic area of concern. My conviction that the church needs to be informed by modern behavioral sciences in order to properly express its mission in the world keeps me involved in my local church, and in what is being done in the behavioral and social sciences generally. And my interest in what the modern clergy need to do and to be involves me in research in pastoral care and counseling and in the meanings of vocational commitments.

Religious writing

These basically professional interests are supplemented by a constellation of sub-professional interests. For example, I am intensely interested in the area of religious writing. Over the past fifteen years I have written and published about a million words in denominational periodicals--from kindergarten

237

up through mature years. For me the attempt to take technical materials in psychology, theology, and education and present them for laypersons in what I hope is a readable form, is an essential form of expression of ministry.

Personal Faith

At present it is not possible for me to list a series of theological statements which constitute a firm foundation of irrefutability. Frankly, the history of humankind's propensity for error has impressed me greatly, so much so that tentativeness has become an integral aspect of my personal faith. I find it possible to be sure, but not cocksure; to be certain enough to act, but not certain enough to proselyte; to be confident enough to risk myself, but not confident enough to demand that others do the same. I am perfectly aware that such a probatory faith is not appreciated by the zealously faithful, that it is often viewed as a weak and poor way to express one's faith. Nevertheless, the tentativeness of my faith is a phenomenological truth, arrived at through many years of searching and even some spiritual agony. It has meant learning to live with ambiguity.

At the same time, St. John's Claim

For God so loved the world that he gave His only Son, that whoever believes in Him should not perish but have eternal life

Is substantial and orientational in my life. Even more so is Jesus' assertion:

You shall love the Lord your God with all your heart, and with all your soul, and with all your mind. This is the great and first commandment. And a second is like it, You shall love your neighbor as yourself.

These scriptural claims, coupled with my experiential validation of them, are enough to cause me to think of Jesus as my Lord and to perceive this lordship in ways which help to determine my experience and behavior.

Still, even these rather substantive statements of faith are received more as mysteries to be lived than truths to be believed. The fact that my personal faith

238

has been influenced more by the life or writings of such persons as St. Francis of Assisi, Simone Weil, Rufus Jones and Evelyn Underhill than from such persons as H. Richard Niebuhr or Paul Tillich is something of a hint as to my propensities in regard to the cognitive explanations of my faith. Probably equally revealing is the fact that I tend to admire psychologists like Gordon W. Allport, Rollo May and Adrian VanKaam more than I do Wilhelm Wundt, J.B. Watson or B. F. Skinner.

Certainly this tendency to appreciate limitations and mystery is also active in my conviction that search is itself a form of faith, and that searching (including waiting), is far more significant than finalized theological statements.

From my Christian perspective, this means that there is much more of God hidden from me than has been revealed to me. But despite this, I do not need to sit back and wait for a full account of His nature and purpose. Part of my personal faith is that in the life death, and resurrection of Jesus Christ I have the best hint as to the nature of the unmanifest. With these faith principles as my anchor points, I choose to move out into reality and form my particular modes of presense and my project of existence.

Integration of Faith and Profession

If one says to me, "Which is more important to you, your faith or your professional life?" I find it exceedingly difficult to answer in any satisfying way. It seems to me that such a question forces over-simplification into an exceedingly complicated picture.

Many years ago, I was having lunch with the late Gordon W. Allport. At the time I was a doctoral can-didate and was representing a seminar of students who wanted me to ask Dr. Allport certain questions about his personality theory. There was one question which I left to last because I had great uneasiness about how it might be received by the Harvard psychologist. The question was: "How much do you think your per-sonal religion has influenced your psychological theories?" When I finally screwed up enough courage to ask this question, Allport looked at me rather sternly and for a swift second I thought he might be thinking of tossing me bodily out of the Harvard

Faculty Club. But then he answered,

> My psychological theories stand on their
> own, no matter my religious faith. On the
> other hand, I think my psychology and my
> faith are of one piece. Unlike some of
> my colleagues, I do not separate my psy-
> chology and my faith into water tight
> compartments.

When I reported this answer back to my seminar,
several of my fellow students did not like this kind of
answer. They wanted to treat faith and psychology as
quite separate things.

But much has happened since that interview with
Allport, and I suspect that many more psychologists
today would be able to understand Allport's desire to
view his faith and his psychological theories as of one
piece.

A lot depends, of course, on one's idea of science.
If we think of science as something "out there," a
body of knowledge existing in its own right, that is
one thing. If, however, we conceive of science as a subjective immersion which moves to a process of reality
checking, that is something quite different.

The Importance of the Human Psyche

I believe one of the important ways God gets himself known in the world is through the operations of
the human psyche as it transacts with the world. Put
another way, it is my firm conviction that the human
psyche is the instrumentation which makes theology
operational in culture.

This is not said in any exclusivistic way. It
does not deny the many other forms of "revelation"
which have been proposed by thinking and feeling persons for centuries. It only says that for me, as a
result of my search and my experiences, it is possible
to come to an understanding of God's actions by attending to the study of the human psyche.

This conviction makes the practice, as well as the
theory, of psychology considerably more than "just
another job" or "something I do for a living" or
"simply another academic field." If I may switch back
to the "typical day" reported on earlier in this

240

chapter, each activity of that day may be viewed in
the faith context of which I have been speaking.

For example--and without going into details of
a confidential nature--the first appointment that
morning was with a man who has suffered some of the
severest kinds of feelings of alienation and guilt.
For months we have been struggling together to find
ways of understanding and feeling what has been
happening to him. In our conversations he has experienced forgiveness and acceptance again and again.
Together we have tried to open ourselves to the be-
friending process, to allow understanding, insight,
and a fuller awareness to become part of our person-
hood.

To me, this process--two persons relating at
many levels of being--is one way in which God's love
finds expression in life. And this is why I sense
that my professional work in this counseling context
is ministry and why faith and profession are fused.

Research As Faith

To illustrate from what may appear to be an
opposite sort of activity, we might note the period in
later afternoon when I became involved in research
activity. Again, my faith is that God continues to
move in the world and, although the mysteries of this
movement may be unimagined by me in my finitude, I do
believe that I have the freedom of search. Indeed, I
am propelled to take quite seriously the process of
search. Research as well as insearch become natural
activities, ones which yield personal satisfaction
and ones which seem to me to be an integral part of my
professional responsibilities.

Most of us cannot conduct research without narrow-
ing it down to areas of limited scope and interest.
For me research tends to direct itself to the study of
the person's religious expressions and their relations
to other life processes. I hope to combine faith and
profession in a fashion which might ultimately assist
others in their searchings.

All of this, I trust, demonstrates how profession
and faith may relate in forms of service and Christian
ministry.

As I read back over what I have written, it
strikes me that there is a sense in which I have avoided professional identity instead of struggling for it.
Frankly, I would find it somewhat sad and not a little
uncomfortable to be identified as psychologist, or
counselor, or professor or clergyman or educational
administrator or writer. Although all of these may be
seen as legitimate professions related to personal
faith, I prefer to think of them as modes of being
moving within the total project of existence.

X.

FACTS AND FANTASIES IN PSYCHOLOGY AND FAITH

There has been an ongoing debate in psychology as to "What's in a name?" Do names such as "Christian Psychologist" stand for anything real? Or are names just labels or tags or signs which help us make distinctions?

One psychologist recently said he was tired of using 'Christian' as an adjective. He personally felt that people who called themselves Christian teachers, Christian lawyers, Christian pilots, or Christian psychologists were using the word in the same way they talked of being from New York or of belonging to the Rotary Club. None of the appendages really make a difference that can be seen. They are like clothes which are worn to make one feel comfortable but which do not change the person underneath.

Of course, the other point of view is that the identity one claims for oneself is the very core of what it means to be a person. This is the contention of this book. However, Dr. Malony takes the unique position in this final chapter that the essence of the difference is an inner rather than an outer matter. The reality of faith may not appear obvious to the casual observer.

Thus, in the final analysis the relationship between faith and such a profession as psychology may be extremely important but subtle.

243

H. Newton Malony is Professor and Director of
Programs in the Integration of Psychology and
Theology in the Graduate School of Psychology of
Fuller Theological Seminary. In addition to being
a clinical psychologist, he is also an ordained
United Methodist minister. He is interested in
helping churches become more affective organizations
and his research is focused in the psychology of
religion. He has published such books as Religious
experience: Its nature and function in the human
psyche (with Walter H. Clark). The Nature of man:
A social psychological perspective (with Richard L.
Gorsuch, and Current perspectives in the psychology
of religion. He is a diplomate in clinical psychology,
the American Board of Professional Psychology.

Psychologist-Christian: A Reality or Just a Label?
by
H. Newton Malony

The first of these essays ended with the observation that knowing who the psychologist Christians were might be a difficult task. It indicated that the only sure means of knowing was to ask the individual psychologist. That essay concluded by suggesting that what persons said they were, they were. Thus, being a psychologist-Christian is auto iographical. It is a confessional stance one takes. Each expression of this inner faith is more than likely an original personal creation.

The foregoing essays appear to be testimonies to this truth, i.e. the unique character of being a psychologist-Christian. Note the divergent themes that appeared. Expressions included the experimental study of values; investigations of the effects of drugs on religious experience; concern with teaching the church how to be more effective; explication of "justification by faith" in psychotherapy; adoption of a stance of openness to new data as a faithing act; sensitivity to persons in administration; establishing a school for teaching a Christian psychology; guiding behavioral expressions of Christian fellowship and personality growth; teaching college students to express their God given selfhood; thinking through the impact of the philosophy of science on theology; stimulation of the church through programs on motivation; writing periodicals and church study materials; ministering through counseling troubled patients in a state hospital; accepting and being revitalized by new experience with God; communicating the gospel message in psychotherapy; and reconsidering the issues of science and religion.

The question remains, however, "Is there such an entity as the psychologist-Christian?" or is the term only a label?

If it is a label which refers to "delimited observables", then even the Vienna circle of philosophers of science would be satisfied and vote to retain the term. This is to say that if it is a term that discriminates between persons who evidence one type of behavior and those who don't it is a functional label and communicates information to those who use it. As to whether the term "psychologist-Christian" does in fact discriminate in this way is uncertain. Much less does this criterion of discrimination between observables decide the question of whether there is beneath the behavior such an entity. We may be attempting in vain to deify a label.

Psychologist-Christian may be like the label "schizophrenia", which is so amorphous it refers to everything and to nothing at the same time. From another viewpoint it may be but a neologism that has served its day or that denotes the private jargonese hope of religious persons. In thinking of these issues at least one psychologist who was invited to contribute to this volume rejected the opportunity and stated "I've no further interest in thinking about the adjectival use of the word Christian or the word psychologist."

It is the contention of this volume that the experience of being a psychologist-Christian is a reality in spite of the fact that it does not always refer to behavior that discriminates between those who do and do not claim the label. As suggested earlier, the expressions of the Christian faith in the profession of psychology are many and varied. As can be seen in the foregoing essays, this self-conscious expression can be within the intrapersonal, professional, experimental, conceptual, or interprofessional aspects of ones life. And within a given area of integration, there will individual interpretations. But in all cases, psychologist-Christians are self-conscious and intentional about their faith, They know and state they are Christians.

It is this last issue of explicit affirmation that guarantees "psychologist-Christian" is a valid

term which stands for a reality. The reality is within. It is attested to and made firm by the verbal
statements of those who claim it as their own.
Humanity's uniqueness is its language, and language
creates each person's reality. The Scriptures state
it thusly "As a man thinketh in his heart, so is he"
(Proverbs 23:7). Psychologist-Christians are those
who say they are. Psychologist-Christians have
made explicit for themselves the ground on which
they stand. They are unashamedly Christian by their
own confession. The task then is not whether, but
how this faith will be expressed. So it is and must
be with Christians who are psychologists.

No claim for completedness is made of these
essays. They are the work of faithing persons in
the midst of their careers. Our hope is that these
descriptions of life styles be stimuli for others
who also desire to integrate their faith and their
professions.

AUTHOR INDEX

249

252